Curing th
Creating your health and life with ease

By Liam Phillips

with major contributions from
Gary Douglas and Dr Dain Heer

This book is copyright. Apart from any fair dealing for the purpose of private study, research, criticism, or review, as permitted under the Copyright Act, no part may be reproduced by any process with out written permission.
Enquires to the author (liamrphillips@yahoo.com).

© Copyright Liam Phillips 2007

First published in Australia 2008 by Luminary Printing
As "Curing the Incurable – Creating health with ease" ISBN: 9780980478303

Rev.Ed. Lulu.com

ISBN: 978-1-4092-4350-2

Front Photo: © Sebastian Kaulitzki - Fotolia.com
Back Photo: © Gordon Issom

Gratitude

The tools given in this book have been developed by Gary Douglas and Dr Dain Heer and practised by Liam and his primary carer Simone (ex wife).

This book is not about how to heal, (that is the realm of your body). It is about the willingness to receive, about creating from consciousness and creating a space for healing to occur.

All of life comes to me with ease, joy and glory!

Many Thanks to:
My Editing Team the Fabulous Simone Phillips, Amazing Cassandra Quirk & the wonderful Yakov Morris
All the Incredible people that featured in the stories
Those two magnificent beings, Dain and Gary
All the Accessories that spent time on my body and facilitating me
To you, the reader
And to my sexy, cute loveable Bod

What if healing was a by product of being conscious?

What else is possible?

Preface

This book is unlike any other you have read on healing. It provides no answer, form or structure. What it does ask is a lot of questions to help you overcome the limitations of your mind and provide you with tools to do this. This book may be an introduction to the rest of your life! Are you willing to go down the rabbit hole? Is it all your fixed points of view and judgements that stop you from fitting down the hole?

"When people choose consciousness, healing is possible."
Gary Douglas

Contents

Introduction…………………………………………………..6

Chapter 1 – Living in the Question………………………….8

Chapter 2 – Ask your Body……………….......................16

Chapter 3 – Talking to your Body………………………..........22

Chapter 4 – Being Grateful……………………………..…...37

Chapter 5 – Allowance………………………………….…..40

Chapter 6 – Interesting Point of View……………………....43

Chapter 7 – Human and Humanoids………………….…...47

Chapter 8 – Judgement……………………………...…..….52

Chapter 9 – What Would It Be Like To Live Without a Story…...57

Chapter 10 – Sex & the Nervous System...……………………..65

Chapter 11 – Hidden Talents and Abilities……………...……...72

Chapter 12 – Expansion……………………………………...74

Chapter 13 – Access Diet…...…………………………………79

Chapter 14 – Energy Work…………………………………..84

Chapter 15 – Caring for People who have a Dis-ease…………….90

Chapter 16 – If It Is Light……………………………………..101

Chapter 17 – The Lost Chapter – The BAC………………105

Postscript and Contact Details……………………………...111

Testimonials

Introduction

Hi, my name is Liam. Shortly after my 39th birthday my body started to act a little differently. For the next 2 years I went on a roller coaster ride with my body that was, to say the least, unpleasant. Okay, that is a lie, it was really horrid. The doctors gave this disease the label of "severe pan ulcerated colitis with dysplastic changes" what a mouthful. In simpler terms it was basically inflammatory bowel disease. As time went by the doctors started to change the diagnosis to all of the above plus ileitis and possibly Crohns. (My spell-check can't even get around some of these words!) During the really horrid parts I was experiencing 20 – 30 runny poohs with excessive mucus (a day), and bleeding from my butt. I had severe cramping and as more blood was lost, other symptoms appeared like falling over and losing weight. At one stage I was down to 42kgs and I stand 186 cm tall! As it progressed I was unable to assimilate food. Picture the prisoners being liberated from Auschwitz and they would look tubby compared to me!

Basically I was starving and bleeding to death. It was torture. Things got increasingly worse and I almost bled to death a few times. After my 41st birthday I made a different choice. I realised I had chosen to create one of the cleverest diseases as it knew exactly how far away I was from a toilet! I am cute but not too bright! I reached the point in the disease where I decided I was not going to be the effect of it any more. I left Australia, wife, work, home and friends, sold everything or gave it away and went to Europe. Basically what I said to myself was that I would not return to Oz until I was healed or I would die on a boat I planned to buy on the Mediterranean.

Whilst in Europe I had intended to write a book that would be my story. However, I never got started. I then made some demands on myself and a bunch of weird, wacky and wonderful people came into my life involved with something called Access. After reading some of their books, having an incredible body session called 'Bars' (which is a simple hands on head process that enabled me to start to unlock a lot of the ideas that were creating my life of dis-ease) with my friend, Angeleta, in England, and doing some courses with Gary and Dain, I asked the question, "What will it take to write this book?" It wasn't long after that that I met the author of "Will Public Speaking be the Death of me?" by Steven James. I told him about my book idea and he asked me a question, "Are you writing it to tell your story or are you writing it to expand consciousness?" This question triggered an awareness for me. It was my intention to tell my story, and it was this very story that locked me into a loop of pain, suffering, dis-ease and unconsciousness.

So, what will it take to write this book to expand consciousness? What are the infinite possibilities?

Chapter 1

Living in the Question

OK, so what's the speed of dark?

At the beginning of my sickness story, especially during the first 18 months, I asked a lot of questions, "Why me? What is the cause of this? What did I do wrong? Why can't anybody help me?" Perhaps you are asking similar questions? These questions look like I was living in the question. They have question marks at the end. They are perfectly good questions to get an answer…right?

When I started Access I recognised that questions like the ones above actually got me stuck in a vicious cycle of pain, suffering and dis-ease. I set myself up as a victim. I chose to give much of my power away to people I thought had the answers, and in so doing I diminished me. I became a victim with a story. I became Liam with the dis-ease rather than Liam the magnificent being I truly am. Are you a victim? Do you have a story to tell? Do you feel trapped in this story?

"Why" questions lend themselves to looking for an answer and it is this very answer that shuts out all the infinite possibilities and opportunities that we live in every day, every moment. The answers that we find stop us from seeing the choices that we are making. They keep us in "victim hood." They keep us in a loop. Every answer becomes a judgement and once you have made a judgement it is like being a horse with blinkers on, you can only see a small piece of the picture.

Imagine looking at the Mona Lisa through an empty toilet paper tube that limits your vision to only a few square centimetres, and then making a critique of the painting based on this. A judgement is like that tube. It will limit your awareness and you will only be able to make limited choices from the answer you thought you had found. The great news is that for every judgement there are 25 other judgements that hold that in place and 25 more that hold each one of those in place, so you can see what a mess your life can become. Why is that great news? Because now you are aware of it. Are you willing to drop judgement and live in the question?

One resistance to dropping judgements, letting go of looking for the answer, of living in the question is; "Who will I be without my story? How will I function in this so-called human reality without my story?" We make a lot of excuses to hang on to our stories. I have met hundreds of people with sicknesses that say, "Okay! That sounds good, I can let go of my story, but…" "But my situation is different" "But my disease is special" "But I am a special case." But…but…but! The only butt you need is the one you sit on! Every time you say "but" it destroys everything you just said. It locks you back into the story. It gives your dis-ease story (or any other story) strength, importance, significance - a life of its own. You become the effect of your story. So…would you like to get off your butts and claim the potency of you?

Who will you be without a story, without a dis-ease story, without judgements, without answers? You will be you, the truly magnificent infinite being you truly are. Will that change your life? Heck, yes! Will friends change, will jobs change, will your partner and loved ones change? Yes!

Some will move on and others will also start to make changes. By being you, you can change the world. Do you want to change your life? What would you like to be, at the mercy of your dis-ease story or the awesome creator of your life?

Some questions that you can use to be the creator of your life, to expand are:
- Who does this belong to?
- What is right about this that I am not getting?
- Where does this come from?
- How did I create this?
- How can it get any better than this?
- Would an infinite being choose this?
- Am I making this significant?
- Is this really mine?
- What will it take to heal?

Let us look at one of these questions in more detail.

"Who does this belong to?"

One of the first things you could do is stop asking "why" questions as they presuppose that you have to find the right answer. Here is some big news. Life has no answers, right or wrong. Could you do that? Instead of asking, "Why do I have these symptoms? Why do I have these obsessive thoughts? Why do I have these feelings of fear, sadness, grief, loneliness, anger etc." you could ask, "Who does this belong to?" If the energy lightens up, or the thought / feeling goes away, or if there is a sudden awareness, a perception of who or where you bought it from, then you know those thoughts or feelings were not yours.

"What?" I hear you say. "If they are not mine then who do they belong to?" Good question! You are very quick! They are the points of view of others that you chose to buy or took on to try to understand where others were coming from. I have a mate that just bought a car. He got a great deal, he is a fantastic creator! When I saw him his car was overheating. A few days later I found out that he had read an article the day before the car overheated, that this particular model had a problem with (you guessed it) overheating! He had taken on that point of view and created from that space.

What if symptoms are your body's way of saying, "I don't need this crap, it's not mine?" What if they are your creations based on points of view that you chose to buy from someone at sometime? A friend of mine (who has the same dis-ease that I had) was practising some verbal processing with me. She asked a very good question, "What comes first, the negative emotion or the symptom?" The old chicken or the egg syndrome (these sayings keep you in a loop, watch out for them!). She is so awesome she knew the reality of this question when I asked her, "What do you know?" She replied "I get stressed when my in-laws are around and my symptoms flare." The emotion comes first, it is something you chose to buy at some time and then you create from that point of view. Therefore for my friend it would be something like this: "My in-laws are coming. Sheesh! That always stresses me out. What if I get sick while they are here?" What does her body hear? "In-laws approaching, please make me sick!" and the body complies. Ouch!

For those of you who are not getting this or who are trying to intellectualize this, here is a little secret. 98% of your thoughts, feelings and emotions are not yours. Still don't get it? Then I'll speak up a bit. **98% of your thoughts, feelings and emotions are not yours!** Are you still avoiding this, thinking this is crazy, intellectualising it, creating a story to hide behind, comparing it, judging it? Then I will yell it out loud, ***98% of your thoughts, feelings and emotions are not yours***. What if the more severe the symptom, the louder your body yelled? Got it?

When I first heard that 98% of your thoughts, feelings and emotions are not yours and let it sink in, I was suddenly hit with a wave of relief. This was a "lightening" of the energy for me. What I got was that a lot of what I thought was mine wasn't, and even though my body was slowly rotting from the inside out, I realised I was creating from thoughts and feelings that were not even mine. (Try reading that sentence again). Yep, you read that sentence correctly. How does it get any better than that?

When you live in the answer, when you are hunting, seeking for a cause for a dis-ease, karmic reasons for the symptoms, the right medication, the right diet…then you become blinkered to the infinite possibilities, you cannot see the whole. Here's an interesting point of view: One definition of healing is to become whole. When you search for a reason for a dis-ease, pain or suffering, then that analysis begins to run your life. When you come from analysis, reason and thought, you are limiting your possibilities of something new turning up in your life. Thought can only come from what you have bought already. If thought was so great, wouldn't you have thought your way out of your dis-ease or story already? When you are willing to receive, the possibilities are infinite. (That's **BIG**!)

"Who does this belong to?" helps to release the thoughts and feelings that trap you in analysis and reason. It opens up the energy. It allows you the willingness to receive and this is the key to healing. If you are unwilling to receive you will stay locked in your story and that story is dis-ease.

Here is a handy little pointer, the "Bars" session that I originally had started to open me up to receiving, something I had stopped doing from all the layers of answers I thought were right, that I had worn like a suit of chain mail.

What are you unwilling to receive that if you were willing to receive would create wholeness? What answers do you have that create the loops of your suit of chain mail that limit your ability to receive? Would you like to take that suit off now?

When you ask the question, "Who does this belong to?" you may find that you perceive a sense of lightness. When this happens it is an awareness that that thought, feeling or pain is not yours. It is something you bought from someone else. If it gets heavy you may have created it. Let's do some math here. If 98% of thoughts, feelings and emotions are not yours, the chances of you finding something that is yours is quite slim. Here is an answer, only 2 % of your thoughts, feelings and emotions are yours (and that's a "maybe" statistic). You have spent years hiding behind these thoughts and feelings, do not worry if they don't lighten up immediately, the power is in the asking of the question…*keep asking.*

Here's a tip, when it lightens up after asking, "Who does this belong to?" you can return it to sender and add "with all the "consciousness of the universe attached to it". I am often asked why you would return it to sender? This allows the person you are returning it to the possibility to expand, to become more aware. To become aware that they don't have to create from a thought or feeling that they bought into as well. What a gift! It also allows you to recognise it was not yours, so you now have the choice to create suffering from that thought or feeling or create something else.

The awesome thing about this little question is you don't have to find the person you bought it from. That would be ridiculous. That would be like one of those "why" questions, where the hunt for the answer traps you into a loop. What you are looking for is an energy.

Tools and Tips
- For any thought, feeling or emotion you can ask the question, "Who does this belong to?"
- For any symptom, pain or disease story you can ask the question, "Who does this belong to?"
- "Why" questions keeps you in the role of victim.
- Looking for reasons or answers to your dis-ease stops you from seeing the infinite possibilities.
- When asking, "Who does it belong to?" if it lightens up it isn't yours.
- When it lightens up, even a tiny, weeny, little bit, return it to sender with all the consciousness of the universe attached to it.
- Here is an example. You have an ache and instead of stating what that pain is, you ask, "Who does this belong to? Where does it come from?" and then "Return to sender with all the consciousness of the universe attached."

- What if the pain or symptom does not lighten up? Then at some point you have bought it as yours. What can you do? Read on, ask more questions.

Please note the words I have used here **'lighten up'.** That does not mean 'disappear' although that may occur. This is not a magic bullet, it is a process of expansion. Please read with awareness, if something does not make sense, put the book down and come back to it later. If something feels heavy, put the book down and come back to it. Or ask a few questions.

Chapter 2

Ask Your Body

How many of you believe in psycho-kinesis? Raise your hand.

Whenever, wherever your body is involved, ask it a question. A friend said, "Who has the time for that?" I do! When I don't, my body yells at me and symptoms appear to increase. My friend's point of view indicates several things. She is not willing to try this and she is also making her story significant. Is my friend sick? Yes! Is she having much fun? No! She is a beautiful being limited by fixed points of view that limit her ability to heal and have fun. I have offered her sessions, she has made it clear that she is unwilling to create change in her life. That is her choice and I must honour that or I will be judging her.

I am very grateful to her. I am also grateful to Dr. Dain Heer for his work with Access, from whose book entitled "Embodiment – The manual that you should have been given when you were born" I gleaned the knowing of asking my body.

Society, culture, family, etc. says we must put others first, we must not take the time to care for ourselves. It is this point of view we have chosen to buy that keeps us controlled, keeps us from creating what we would like in our lives. Wherever you make something significant, important or serious, you expend huge amounts of energy defending that point of view. Energy that could be used in healing, being conscious.

Whatever dis-ease story or symptom you are making significant, are you willing to destroy and uncreate it?

Wherever you have put other people's needs or wants before asking what your body would like, are you willing to destroy and uncreate all that and listen to your body?

"What is this destroy and uncreate thing?" I hear some of you ask. Excellent question! It is a willingness to change a thought pattern. It does not mean you have to destroy something physically, it is simply your willingness to be aware that you have been operating from an old program that no longer serves you, and that you are now willing to choose something different.

This works! I took a client shopping recently to practise the question, "Body, what would you like to wear?" This guy hadn't been clothes shopping in years. He had been too busy working as the CEO of his company. We didn't go shopping to spend money, we went to practise questions and have fun. The first shirt he picked was okay, a blue stripy polo, the second shirt was similar but not quite as smart. The choices he was making were coming from past reference points, what he always wore. He said he liked blue stripes, there wasn't much enthusiasm or joy in his voice and he had started to justify his reasons for choosing. I asked him if he would be willing to destroy and uncreate all his reasons and justifications for picking clothes?" "Yes" was his answer. I said "Look around and when something catches your eye, when your body is drawn to something totally different, have a look at that." This guy was so willing to be a conscious leader that the next shirt he picked up was the one his body wanted. Black, short sleeved, soft cloth. Very sexy! "I wouldn't normally go for black or something with such short sleeves." said my friend. He was starting to give me reasons for why this shirt was no good. "Whoa, I said, try it on, see if your body likes it." He then tried to weasel his way out of it, "I'll have to look for my size." I said, "Your body is conscious, it picked this shirt, it picked the right size." He tried it on. Guess what? It was the right size! He came out of the changing rooms and these were his words, "Wow! This is a BMW shirt." We laughed as we held up the original "Ford" shirt next to the sexy Beamer shirt. He bought the shirt on the spot and didn't even look at the price tag. His body knew what looked good on him. It even knew there was 30% off the price tag too! How does it get any better than that?

We laughed all the way home, it was so much fun. It was light and easy. Trust your body, ask your body. Thank you.

"Great story! I hear you say, but my body is in pain. It's dis-eased. How is buying a shirt going to help me?" When was the last time you asked your body what it would like? When I asked my body what it would like, it rejoiced. The week I started asking my body I put on 5kgs, in 3 weeks I put on a total of 10kgs, which was also the week that I had received my first life changing 'Bars' session. Before I started I was less than 50kgs and I stand 186cm tall. (For our American friends, that is over 6 feet tall and less than 90 pounds!) I was puffed out climbing 2 flights of stairs. In 4 weeks I walked up Goatfell Mountain on the Isle of Aran in Scotland, which is 822m high and very steep. In 6 weeks I was walking up to 18kms a day in the Sierra Nevada in Spain. My libido returned. Men and women have remarked at how well I look, and I am willing to receive it. The more I honour my body by being willing to receive its wisdom, by asking it questions, a stronger, more energetic, better looking, sexier body appears as if by magic. How does it get any better than that? Did I ask it what shirt it would like to wear? Yes! What it wanted to eat? Yes! What I didn't do was to fill it with food, medication, exercise, meditation, supplements, work, sex, etc. that it didn't want. What I didn't do was shove everyone else's point of view on it and in it.

How was this achieved? It is so simple that your mind may well be unable to grasp it. What if all the points of view that you have to do something to become healthy, limit your body's ability to heal? When there is respect and a willingness to listen to your body, then you create space for more possibilities, more choices to turn up. How cool is that? Does creating space make you feel lighter? What have you got to lose? You think you have tried everything otherwise you wouldn't be reading this, so give it a go. Ask your body if it would like to be asked, "Body, would you like me to ask you about you?" Give it choices. How do you react when someone commands you to do something? What happens when someone makes a request of you? Which is more fun? The latter, right? So, would this be the same with your body?

I here a "but" question. That is so cool, every "but" is an opportunity to expand. "But what if there are things that you must do? Like work?" You can always ask your body, "How can I make this more comfortable for you?" Or you could ask other questions like; "Do I really have to do this job? What are the possibilities of doing this differently?"

What I also found out later about the 'Bars' session was that it helped me unlock many of the limitations, or points of view that were holding my disease in place. It also prepared me for receiving. It enabled me to receive my body's wisdom. How does it get any better than that?

Do I still continue with these 'Bars' sessions? You bet! Every time I give one or receive one I access more of me, and not only that, I get as much hands-on Access body processes as I can. For what reason would I not?

When you ask your body it responds with all the enthusiasm of a beloved pet. The body is an animal and when you give it attention, when you touch it, listen to it, let it play, when you care and nurture it, it will always respond joyfully.

What does health mean to you? Are you willing to unlearn every point of view that you have ever bought about health and listen to your body? Including that one that chocolate is fattening?

A Diary of Shulfi the Dog
8:00 am - Dog food! My favourite thing!
9:30 am - A car ride! My favourite thing!
9:40 am - A walk in the park! My favourite thing!
10:30 am - Got rubbed and petted! My favourite thing!
12:00 pm - Lunch! My favourite thing!
1:00 pm - Played in the yard! My favourite thing!
3:00 pm - Wagged my tail! My favourite thing!
5:00 pm – Bones! My favourite thing!
7:00 pm - Got to play ball! My favourite thing!
8:00 pm - Wow! Watched TV with the people! My favourite thing!
11:00 pm - Sleeping on the bed! My favourite thing!

What is your favourite thing to do? And if you are not doing it or being it, would that impact on your body? Would doing things that you loathe to do impact your body?

Would you like to know how to commune with your body and allow your body to heal? I don't think I am going to tell you. It is too easy. It requires no science, no mind, no analysis, no energy and no money (this tool has saved me thousands of dollars). It is such a simple tool, I have given it its own chapter.

Tools and Tips
- Whenever, wherever your body is involved, ask it a question.
- Are you shoving other people's points of view into your body?
- Are you putting other people's feelings before your body?

Chapter 3

Talking with your Body

On the other hand, you have different fingers.

What Dain recommends and I have experienced with delight is this: if it involves your body ask it! IF IT INVOLVES YOUR BODY ASK IT! It is amazing the number of people don't get this so I'm going to say it again, IF IT INVOLVES YOUR BODY ASK IT! Wherever you are unwilling to receive this message for whatever reason will you destroy and uncreate that now? Thank you!

I am willing to give you 10 minutes of my time for free and the first thing I will ask you is, "Are you checking in with your body?" and if you say "No," or "Sometimes," or come up with an excuse like, "I can't do this because I can't trust my body's response, because I can override it." I will tell you to go away and start to give your body some choice, that is, start to ask your body what it would like.

Here is a tool for those of you who will come up with excuses like the one above. This tool will help you unlock your body's wisdom which you have suppressed with all those points of view that you bought. The reason you are in this mess to begin with is because you have NOT listened to your body. If you know you can override it, then you know when you are doing it, because if you didn't use this excuse, you wouldn't know you could override it and that excuse wouldn't even come up! And if you go "der" after that sentence, you might like to read it again because it was written especially for you. It is a choice, and this excuse is a choice that you are making that keeps you in your story and your unwillingness to change. So, please don't lie to yourself. You know when you are doing that, it's just that you are making excuses and your story more significant than you. Oh and because I'm psychic (some may say psychotic!), the excuse about being self conscious when you do this in public just isn't going to wear with me. I tried that one myself!

Most people are so caught up in their own stories they won't even see you. I bet you are one of those people who seem to be overlooked or bumped into anyway, because you have the ability to vibrate at such a different speed that some people just can't see you. Some people are going to judge you as weird. (Hey, people can have their own point of view, that is called allowance!) I bet you are a bit different to others anyway, so what is new. The others are going to ask you a question and it is those people who are going to get some awareness from you. How cool is that? By asking your body you create the possibility of changing the reality of another person. (What are the implications of that for our planet?) It is also those people who are going to be potential buddies.

Would you like to heal? Become whole? Be conscious? Is it possible that by asking your body you could facilitate this?

Does this include where it would like to go? Yes! The job it would like to do? Yes! The food it likes to eat? Yes! The person it has sex with? Definitely yes! Supplements, medications, surgery, exercise? Yes, yes, yes! In truth if it involves your body, ask it first. Of course, if you are standing in traffic, there is no need to use a tool to ask your body because your body will be screaming at you to move!

For what reason would you be standing in traffic in the first place? Would it be because you hadn't asked your body where it would like to go? In other words when you are in a life threatening situation with your body, your body will be willing to move out of that situation as quickly as possible, and the only reason your body would be in that situation is because you haven't been aware and listened to it. Hey, does that sound like a definition for disease/healing? Interesting point of view.

Your body has its own consciousness. It doesn't have thoughts or emotions, things that humans prize so highly, to distract it. So you can actually trust it when it comes to choices regarding itself. It is true to you. It likes living. It loves sex. It craves movement and it enjoys touch. It was designed for all that. Where have you bought the point of view that the body is a worthless bag of meat that needs to be transcended, or cleansed, or has no consciousness, or is a sin, or is wrong? Would you like to destroy and uncreate those beliefs, please?

Your body won't put you in harms way. It will always get you to where you would like to go. Even if you are unable to move your body, have you ever noticed it is always with you (at least when you're awake)? Even when you treat it like a bag of shit? How often before and during disease have you blamed your body, judged the hell out of it? Truth... even that subtle, sneaky little judgement about hair colour or the size of an appendage? Can you imagine what it would be like to live with a person that judged your body the way you judge yours? Perhaps you do. Do you think that relationship would be healthy? And the right answer is...? (And if you are looking for a right answer, are you making a judgement?) Delete that! Please don't imagine anything, there has been enough judging as it is. There wasn't a day that went by that I didn't judge my body as being too skinny. Funny that I should end up with a disease where my body was disappearing! So are you willing to give up every, every, every, every, every, every, every, every judgement (to the Nth degree) you have ever had about your cute little bod?

You may have bought the point of view that the symptoms of disease are your body's way of screaming at you. (Yeah, I know I am contradicting what I wrote earlier, that's the thing with awareness, when one makes it concrete it becomes a system, an answer, and then the energy stops.) What if these symptoms are actually awarenesses that you are unwilling to receive? What if they are the result of the thoughts and emotions that you chose to buy at some point. Are you willing to perceive and receive those awarenesses?

The great thing about asking your body is the asking. This empowers you and your body. When you are <u>told</u> to do something, is there often a resistance, that you are not really thought of very highly, of superiority and inferiority? So when you make your body do things without asking, what do you think your body perceives? When you are asked to do something do you usually go, "Okay I have been asked, I have a choice here, I can do that easily." So when you ask your body, when it has a choice, how will it respond? Please review the dog's diary if you are seeking an answer.

Are you willing to ask your body questions? Are you willing to allow your body to heal itself? All the stories, all the attention you get and all the significance of your disease, are you willing to destroy and uncreate that totally? Thank you!

I hear some of you asking "Will this work with my kids?" Are your kids conscious? Do they know things that you have forgotten? Your kids will get this better than you. Any of these tools, your kids will get better than you. Except teenagers, of course, they will get it, but if it ain't cool they will snub it. So how can you make it cool? Will kids try to manipulate you with this? Yes! If you are invested in the outcome it won't work.

Let me steal one of Gary's stories about a child who used this technique. He said to his Mum, "My body wants ice cream for breakfast." "Okay!" Mum said. This happened a few more times, and on the third or fourth time the kid got the idea that he could manipulate the situation and eat whatever he wanted. So the next time he asked for ice cream, Mum said, "Yes!" and he promptly threw up. Did he go against his body's knowing? Yes! His Mum had the willingness to allow her child to play with this. She knew he was an infinite being with a little body and allowed him to choose. That empowered the child. Do you want to empower your child? Have you bought the idea that ice cream is not a breakfast item? What if your body knew what was best for it and when? Would your child's body have the same knowing?

Stand with your feet together, heel to heel, toe to toe. Hold whatever it is you would like to digest (listen to, watch, dress in …) in front of you level with your solar plexus. Ask the question, 'Body, would you like to digest (listen to, watch, wear…) this ………?"

Let us stop there and play with this. (If you are unable to stand you can modify this, for example, sit with feet together etc.) Get something you think you would like to eat, listen to, dress in… and ask your body the question, "Body, would you like to digest, listen to, dress in ………?"

Now having done that, what did you notice about your body. Did it move? Did it move toward the object you are holding i.e. forward? Was it intense? (Did you almost fall over?) Or was it subtle? (Barely moved). Did it move away from the object, i.e. backward? Did it move to the side? There is no right or wrong here, you will not be marked or judged. Perhaps there was no movement? Perhaps you sensed something different, a lightness or a heaviness?

I wrote this on 2 April 2007 when there was an earthquake in the Pacific, and the east coast of Australia was expecting a Tsunami. I was completely unaware of this. I woke with no sense of "I have got to go to the mountains today for a walk in the forest!" I asked my body, "What would you like to do this morning?" I ran through a few things including a walk in the hills. It said, "Gym." When I arrived at the gym I found out a Tsunami may be approaching. I live 50m from the beach. I asked my body, "Do you want to go back home?" "No!" was the reply. The gym is on the third floor of a large hotel so my body knew something. Either the wave wasn't coming or I would be safer in the gym than in my ground floor flat. I continued with my gym session which body loved. No Tsunami hit. My body will not lie to me. It likes living!

What I would like you to do is try this with a few things. To ask questions of your body and see which way it moves. Maybe you could do this with 10 different things? Maybe you could do it till you get some response from your cute little bod? Have some fun. Don't read ahead for an answer, you'll just shoot yourself in the foot with expectation.

What I would like you to do is get a sense of how your body talks to you. In all probability, if you have a disease or a body image issue, it is because you have not been listening to your body for a long time. Put the book down for a while if necessary, and just use this technique with everything. Play with it. Have fun with it.

I hear a few of you say, "Oh, this is just muscle testing…" There is no test here. There is no right or wrong. There is no comparison. It is about you reconnecting with your body. About communion. About stepping outside your box called the mind. Are you willing to step out of all that you think you know and listen to what your body has to say? Your body is jumping for joy when that willingness is there. I have highlighted part of this text for those of you who want to be 30 steps ahead of where you are now. Yes, I am talking directly to you!

Here's a tip. Do you close your eyes when you ask your body? Would an infinite being need to close their eyes to perceive energy? When you close your eyes are you receiving more or shutting things out? If closing your eyes works for you, what are you going to do? The reason I ask these questions is to make you aware of what you have bought.

I asked a client about closing his eyes, and he tried it with eyes open and with eyes closed. His response was, "That is great! I always bought the idea that to receive more I have to close my eyes. That always felt a bit heavy for me." He went on further to say, "Now I won't look so weird when I ask my body what it would like in a restaurant!"

Talking of restaurants…when I started this I was in Scotland with a lady friend who I wanted to impress, and because I felt embarrassed I would duck into the loo to ask my body what it would like to eat! I would memorise the menu and excuse myself (as if I had not spent enough time in the toilet over the past 2 years, bowel disease is like that!) pop out, pop back in, make my order! Well, since I am psychic I got the sense that this lady was catching on after a few days, especially when I would perform the same operation for dessert. So in the middle of a crowded pub, I explained what I was doing with my little trips to the loo, and with lots of ceremony, I then stood up and proceeded to ask my body what it would like from the menu. We cracked up! No-one noticed, she was very interested, and the next day she really opened up. How does it get any better than that? Be you and change the world!

The reason I ask you to do this a few times without knowing the answer to your question, "What does it mean when the body moves forward…?" is so your mind can't override your body and make your body do what it wants. In so doing we destroy your next excuse, "This doesn't work, I just overrode my body." Are excuses just you weaseling out, not wanting to change? Some of you have already bought the idea that if the body moves in a certain way it means this or that. Any beliefs that you have about your mind overruling your body, or a particular movement means a specific thing, or that your body needs this because of such and such a reason, would you be willing to destroy and uncreate all that now?

Congratulations for doing this. You are now on the way to being in communion with your body.

Here's an interesting point of view. Did your body move forward, backward or to the side with different things? Did it, at different times with the same thing move in different ways? Well, here's what you have been waiting for. If the body moves forward towards the object, it means "yes" to your question. If the body moves backwards away from the object, it means "no", and if it moves to the side, it means "please ask a different question." If you sense a lightness, that would also be a "yes." If you sense a heaviness, that would be a "no" or an indication for you to ask more questions. A very intense response would be a definite "yay" or "nay." If you are unsure ask more questions.

One client who was shown this technique used this on his HIV medication. The first two questions he asked, his body moved to the side, the third question he asked, his body moved forward so intensely he almost fell over. His body was happy to receive the energy of the medication at that time. Interesting point of view! He had a strong resistance to using medication. We did a few clearings and his body confirmed that medication was okay at that moment. How does it get any better than that?

Wherever, whenever you have decided to align and agree with or resist and react to a point of view regarding medication, food, supplements or exercise are you willing to destroy and uncreate all that now? Thank you.

By destroying and uncreating preconceived ideas, beliefs, reasons and thoughts you start to create an empty space where you are capable of receiving infinite possibilities, and you start to receive the body's knowing. You start to commune with it rather than push it around. Yes, I recognise

I have already mentioned this. I have written it again for that other person that missed it the first time round.

Asking questions of your body is honouring it, including it. By including it you allow consciousness to expand. Asking questions creates awareness. Ask more questions of your body and awareness of your body will expand, and you will have a greater capacity to create the body you would like. You give your body the opportunity to change. Would you like to do that? I know your body would.

You can have lots of fun with your body using this technique. Here's another story. One night in Glasgow during Halloween, my body had chosen some penguins to eat (choc coated biscuits sold in the UK, not the bird, though I'm sure they are tasty too!) I could only buy them in packs of 18, my body only wanted 2, so it was fun to share this abundance with the homeless and musos (for our brothers and sisters in other countries, Australians like to shorten words and often add an "ie" or 'o' at the end of a word, so musician becomes "muso," vegetable becomes "vegie" etc.) After a while the goodies ran out and having nothing else to do, I asked my body, "Would you like to walk?" "Yeah." Okay, so I would ask it at every crossroad, "Which way?" Whichever way my body would lean was the way we went. Once I asked, "Which way bod?" My body leaned backwards with such intensity I almost fell over. So we about-faced and went back the way we came. "Weird, I thought, "we are going in bloody circles, what's all this about?" I looked up and saw a sexy woman in front of me, she was sucking energy like crazy and my body had picked this up. Funny thing was that her boyfriend could've been my brother, he looked so similar. Then the bell rang! Hey, my body is playing! Play has no reason, that is why I had judged this as weird and why it took my mind so long to pick this up. Life is playful. If it isn't, you are doing pain, suffering and gory. My body was playing like a child. It had no reason to "do", it was just being and it has this amazing ability to get me where I have to be by following the energy. I felt very light, and if it is light it is true for you.

Have you ever seen those docos (TV documentaries) about birds migrating thousands of miles, and then the narrator spins a story about how they do this and how science has proved it. What if those birds just follow the energy? What if they are just aware? What would happen if we were able to tell them the scientific reason for their amazing ability? Would they fall of their perches in laughter? Would some of them buy the story and get lost?

Where have you bought a reason, scientific evidence, or a story for your disease and gotten lost? Do you sometimes buy your own story as real? Would you be willing to destroy and uncreate all these stories about disease?

Do you look for reason in everything you do? Do you impose that reason on your body? Do you have a life purpose as a reason for living? Would you like to give that up? Have you gone somewhere and met someone supposedly by chance and that meeting changed your life or provided you with the next step? Perhaps this book turned up in your life like that. Who got you to that place, your reason, or your body? Or a question? The more you ask questions of your body the more you are saying to your body, "Wow! You are so cool! What else is possible, buddy?" What other hidden talents and abilities do you have that you have decided to hide? Would you be willing to destroy and uncreate everywhere you have hidden yourself?

What are your body's talents and abilities? Would you like to claim, own and acknowledge your body's talents and abilities?

Before disease I was a yoga teacher, an organic-only food buff, a meditation guru, a health freak. I pushed and shoved my body with reason. I forced my body to eat things it hated because I had bought the point of view that I knew better, it was more healthy, and I was doing it for its own good. I crippled myself into full Lotus position and then bounced my base chakra "Mulladah" on the floor 20 times to achieve Nirvana (I achieved aching knees and a sore asshole!) I'd escape from life and my body for hours at a time and call it meditation! I'm sure you get the picture. I was killing my body with reason, judgement and thinking. I thought I knew better than my body (that thinking thing can be dangerous!) It happened with drugs in my younger days. It happened with medication, with health supplements, with sex. I thought I knew best for my body. I knew crap!

Thinking is stinking (very appropriate for bowel issues!) I laugh every time I read this paragraph. How many kangaroos do you know that hop into the local health food shop for vitamins? None, right? Do you think they might follow the energy by allowing their body to take them to the grasses that supply them with what their body requires? It's all crap. It's not that vitamins or meditation or whatever, are crap. It's your point of view and judgement about these things that are crap. Are you willing to function from no point of view? To commune with your body and ask its wisdom, ask it questions? Are you willing to receive from your body? Sometimes body says, "Yes." and sometimes, "No." And if body says, "No thanks, not today," what do you do then? Do you give some reason, some point of view you chose to buy from someone else and pop the vitamins anyway? Or do you say, "Thanks body, I'm so grateful to you." and give it what it would like? Did you know you can always ask another question or ask again later?

Part of disease we often make significant is the "unknowing." Often that is misidentified as emotional stress. A lot of "what if" and "why" questions come up as you struggle for an answer, cure or cause. Asking your body is a cool tool to use. It takes all that energy you have locked into your body as stress, emotion, feeling, pain and suffering and releases it for other things. It is at this point that the body has the opportunity to start healing itself. Having bowel issues I chose to buy the point of view that the food I ate was very significant. In short, I was obsessed with food. Who did this belong to? Check out some of the books on bowel disease and you'll see where I bought these ideas from and you know what? I don't always consciously go, "okay I will buy that one." Sometimes it appears to be unconscious, sometimes it is to prove a point of view, sometimes it is because I see that idea three times in a row. Well, it just has to be true then, doesn't it? I spent most of my time thinking about, buying, preparing and eating food. Not much time for anything else. Coming down the mountain in Scotland I realised that when I asked my body about food I no longer needed to obsess about food. When I got hungry I could just ask my body what it would like. That little realisation took so much stress and obsessive thought out of my life that I had so much more energy available for my body. Cool eh? Asking your body can alleviate all the hunting, looking for a cure, an answer or a cause. You start living more and more from moment to moment. It's so simple! I bet you don't do it! What are your reasons for not listening to your body? Whatever they are, are you willing to destroy and uncreate those now? Your body is very grateful!

Give your body a choice and it is usually pretty happy. The power is in asking the question. What you are saying in posing a question to your body and to the universe is "I am grateful to you, I am willing to receive from you." Are you willing to allow your body the luxury it enjoys, to let it play and have fun?

Let's lighten this up a little. Here is a joke (a joke is another point of view) regarding advice from a doctor to a patient:
Patient: "Should I cut down on meat and eat more fruit and vegetables?"
Doctor: "Look at this logically. What does a cow eat?"
Patient: "Grass and hay."
Doctor: "And what are these?"
Patient: "Green leafy vegetables."
Doctor: "So a steak is nothing more than an efficient mechanism of delivering vegetables to your system! Need some grain? Eat chicken! Beef is a good source of field grass (green leafy vegetable)! And pork can give you 100% of your recommended daily allowance of vegetable products!"

Tools and Tips
- Stand with your feet together, heel to heel, toe to toe. Hold whatever it is you would like to digest (listen to, watch, dress in …) in front of you level with your solar plexus. Ask the question, 'Body, would you like to digest (listen to, watch, wear this ………?"
- If the body moves forward toward the object this means "Yes" to your question, backward, away from the object, means "No" and to the side, "Please ask a different question."
- Honour what your body says and you start to create communion and ease.
- You can always ask more questions and ask again later.
- If it involves your body, ask it!
- Would you like to heal, become whole, be conscious? Then ask your body.
- This includes where it would like to go, the job it would like to do, the food it likes to eat, the person it has sex with, supplements, medications, surgery, exercise…Yes! You are absolutely right, I am teasing you with these words, EVERYTHING.

Chapter 4

Being Grateful

Thank you

We say we are grateful. We say we are being grateful. We don't say we do grateful. Gratitude is not a doing, it is a beingness. How often do you express gratitude to your body? When everything is okay with it, we basically ignore it. Is that gratitude? When it speaks to us with pleasurable sensations we often say thank you to the person or thing that instigated that sensation, but do not thank our bodies. Was that person or thing the cause of that sensation? When it speaks to us with pain, we often judge it or ignore it or take an aspirin. Is this gratitude? When we ask a question of the body we are acknowledging it. Could there be gratitude in acknowledgement? Could we be more grateful to our bodies? Gratitude is a key to a happy, vibrant body and life. Wherever, whenever you have ignored, judged, or suppressed your beautiful body, are you willing to destroy and uncreate that?

There may be some of you who make those judgements etc. significant. Okay, so you may have been treating your body like shit in the past, so choose again. There is no need to make more story out of it. That story is a contraction of you. It is keeping you in the box, locking out all the infinite possibilities. Instead, you could destroy and uncreate all that and now choose to listen to it. Wherever, whenever you make more story about being wrong, would you be willing to destroy and uncreate all that?

Hey, look! Now is a good time to pat yourself on the back, or if your body would prefer it, a hug or a tickle or…and recognise that just by reading this book and being willing to destroy and uncreate, you are taking the first steps to a body of ease. How does it get any better than this?

Recently I found myself running late for a business meeting. Whilst driving there I recalled that I had forgotten some documents, so I returned to the office for them. Once I had collected these documents I took off, rushing to get to the meeting. My body was saying, "I am very hot." All I could think of was to take my jacket off. To do this, it would have been necessary to pull over. I said to body, "It's only 5 minutes away, you can wait." I was prepared to go back to get documents. I was prepared to put the business meeting before my body. Was there any gratitude in that? Was I putting me first, my body, or was I choosing for money, for the other person? I managed to ask a question, something like, "How can I cool down?" I then had the realisation to turn the AC on. Body was then happy. I am very cute but not too bright!

Wherever, whenever you have asked a question of teachers, parents, friends, or other people you have made significant, and they have belittled you and wherever you have squashed others for asking questions and decided never to ask silly questions again. Will you destroy and uncreate that? Wherever you have decided that you will only ask questions you have the answer to or that you will never ask a question, would you be willing to destroy and uncreate all that? You guys are hard work.

Tools and Tips
- Gratitude is a key to a happy, vibrant body and life.
- Asking questions is being grateful.
- Being Grateful is not a doing it is a way of being.
- Generosity of spirit and gratitude will change your reality.
- The question "How does it get any better than that?" will start to create more gratitude in your life. It can be used in any circumstance, good, bad or ugly.

Chapter 5

Allowance

Allowance is not a door mat

Remember, half the people you know are below average.

It is not about throwing out medication or resisting surgery or stopping exercise or not following a diet…it is about asking questions. You can ask your body or the universe any question regarding your health. For example, what would it take for a nurturing diet to show up for my body? Ask the question and the universe and your body will get you to the person, the book, the TV show, or whatever, that can help. Are you willing to toss out all your fixed points of view about health and ask your body? It is your body that will get you to where you are required to be.

Have you noticed when the body is healing, you sleep a lot. What if sleep was so you could get out of your body's way, so it can do what it does best without any intervention from you? How does it get any better than that? During dis-ease you may feel sleepy a lot. Do you allow your body to sleep or do you fight it, push it and deny it? Wherever you believe that being sleepy or sleeping often is an indication that you are a lazy asshole, would you be willing to give that up, destroy and uncreate that? Yahoo!

Do you know why women don't blink during foreplay, because they don't have time!

Wherever you resist and react to something, like that joke, you have a fixed point of view about something. What if in that 10 seconds of unconsciousness that you buy a point of view helps to create the pain, suffering and disease in your life? Or perhaps you accept the point of view of the joke as true, and align and agree with it. You have then just come from a space of unconsciousness, or you have just collected data to justify that point of view to make you right. Wherever you have decided to be right and defend your point of view would you like to throw that out? Yippee!

Would an example be of assistance here? I was of the point of view that I could beat the disease I had with diet and meditation. I resisted and reacted to medication for a long time. I became very sick. Medication helped, and then I started to accept or align and agree with the doctors that medication was the way, and then interestingly, the medication stopped working! In both cases I did a lot of research to justify my point of view. I became a guru of the disease and in so doing I started to create the symptoms more and more. When I came from anything but allowance, whenever I tried to make my body a testing ground for my beliefs, I would get sick. What an awesome creator. Cute, but not too bright!

Wherever you have made your body a testing ground for other people's points of view by aligning and agreeing or resisting and reacting to them, would you be willing to destroy and uncreate all that? Would you be willing to be in complete allowance of your body and other people's points of view? For those of you who are already asking the question, "How do I do that?" the next chapter gives you the tool to do that very thing. How does it get any better than that? Congratulations to those of you who are starting to ask questions. Can you see how asking the question provides you with the next step?

Tools and Tips
- Are you resisting and reacting to something?
- Are you aligning and agreeing with someone's point of view?
- Will doing either of these make you feel lighter?

Chapter 6

Interesting point of View

Eagles may soar, but weasels don't get sucked into jet engines.

This book was originally intended for people who created <u>I</u>nflammatory <u>B</u>owel <u>D</u>isease (IBD) (hence the many references to shit) or what I now call <u>I</u>nsane <u>B</u>ody <u>D</u>estruction. Once the question, "What will it take to write this book from consciousness?" was asked, I perceived how limiting my original intention was. These tools can be used for any dis-ease. What if I were to tell you that we are the creators of our lives? That we buy into all the points of view we have heard or read or seen or remembered at sometime, that we choose the beliefs that shape our lives that we call ours, including all the spiritual points of view. We create our own dis-eases. We choose the dis-ease that will somehow support our beliefs. Yep, the cause of all disease is us. Wherever you have chosen a disease to prove your point of view and that includes this point of view, would you like to give that up?

It is very liberating to know that you are the creator of your dis-ease. "Nope!" I hear some of you say. Well, hang on a moment! Are you willing to claim, own and acknowledge what an awesome creator you are? That you can actually create such a change in your body? Is that not good news! You bet it is, because it means you can choose again!

Here is another tool to enable you to cut away resisting and reacting or agreeing and aligning with something (which is saying to your body "I don't trust you.") It is called

interesting point of view. Perhaps you have just come from your specialist and they have suggested that it is time to have your bowel removed. You can align and agree with them and then you are going to loose a beautiful part of your body, or you can resist and react, which will initiate your fight-flight response. (No wonder your adrenals are overworked and you are feeling stressed, and your liver function is all over the place and…) Or you could say or think, "Interesting point of view**,** Doc. What else is possible?" Ask your body if that would be appropriate. And it is not just the so called 'biggies' that you can use "interesting point of view" with. It is for anything. The used-car salesman says, "Don't bother checking the Redbook (An on-line car evaluation service). "Interesting point of view, mate!" The thing with points of view is that you have bought so many of them that you think they actually belong to you. They are at the root of the thoughts and feelings that you think you have. They are your beliefs and it is these beliefs that are creating dis-ease. You are the creator of your disease, of your financial situation, of your life. Would you be willing to claim and own and acknowledge that you are the creator of all your life situations?

Wherever someone pushes your buttons, you have a fixed point of view. You will have a ton of justifications as to why they are wrong or right. This is an ideal time to use this tool "interesting point of view." There is no need to go digging up rubbish that you have bought, it will come up naturally in your daily life. That's when to use the tools. The great thing about the dis-ease that you created is that you are going to get lots of opportunities to use these tools, and so you are going to have more possibilities to become more aware, more whole. Would you like that? These tools are like mix and match clothes, you can mix and match them and have even more fun whilst you are healing. When you have practised "interesting point of view" with a few people, you can try it on all the thoughts that you become aware of, and add on "that I had that point of view." For example: "Interesting point of view I had that point of view", and then tag on a "Who does that belong too?" I tell you, you are going to have so much fun healing you might not want to give it up! You may make it into another story. Would you be willing to give up all that crap? Thank you.

Here is an example of how quickly a point of view can be bought and how much power we can give them. A friend was given the diagnosis of Colitis by her doctor, who then suggested that it was no big deal, that this would only last a few years. She bought that point of view and the dis-ease was no big deal and it only lasted for few years. Any point of view we buy has the potential to run our life, whether it is good or bad. By using interesting point of view we step out of that game altogether. What is also interesting about this story is that the Doctor did not make the dis-ease significant. Perhaps he was aware of what he was saying. What if we were all aware of what we were creating with what we say, and think?

A client once said, exasperated, "If I use interesting point of view with every thought, feeling and emotion, I'm not going to have a point of view." I looked at him and we laughed and laughed. The whole point is not to have one (point of view that is). When you lack a point of view on something, whether it is the weather, child rape, or a disease, there will be no emotional charge to store in your body to make it sick. Interesting point of view, Liam! Would you like to stop holding all those points of view in your body? Body sighs with relief. Thank you! Next chapter!

Tools and Tips

- Use "interesting point of view", to come into allowance of all points of view for 12 months.
- You can use all the tools, mix and match.
- Don't beat yourself up when you forget to use the tools, that is just an interesting point of view.
- Interesting point of view is not a weapon against someone or a shield with which to defend your belief.
- When we do not make things significant and we are aware of what we say and think, we can be the affect of life. Interesting point of view will get us to this space if you are willing. If you are a carer or professional would that make a difference to peoples lives?

Chapter 7

Humans and Humanoids

Light travels faster than sound. That's why some people appear bright until you hear them speak.

Have you seen the Triple J advert on TV? Triple J is an alternative music station in Australia. Their logo is a drum with 3 drumsticks. Their latest advert on TV is a pencil drawn person with no arms hitting his head on a drum making simple drumming sounds. Then an arm grows on one side clutching a drum stick. He starts playing a drum lick. Then a second arm sprouts and the drum lick gets better. At this point I went, "Cool, how does it get any better than that?" Then a third arm grows from his chest and the drum lick is awesome. My experience of people is that we have 2 arms. This ad showed me that there are other possibilities, and often our experience is a limitation as to what else is possible.

It happened in the gym the other day when my body said it wanted to bench press a heavier weight. In my experience I had never pushed that weight before. I immediately started to doubt this. What was I creating? Limitation? I used the tools from Access that I know and my body pushed the weight. How can it get better than that?

Are you creating expansion or limitation when you say "in my experience?" I have a network marketing business and I often hear people say that they have tried network marketing in the past and 'in their experience' it doesn't work. Is this true? Are they creating a limitation? Have they made a judgement? Was it actually their limited points of view that they bought, that created the original experience that network marketing companies don't work? If you have had experiences with therapies, medication, food, etc. that have not worked in the past, is it true for you now? What tools could you use to be willing to receive the infinite possibilities? Interesting point of view? Ask a question? What else is possible? So are you more like the Triple J drummer with three arms or are you a human with the standard issue of two arms? Could dis-ease be an opportunity to change? To step up to who you really are? A metamorphism to allow you to access the talents and abilities that you have hidden?

You are reading this book because you think you have exhausted all possibilities. I am here to tell you that you have only just started opening the door to infinite possibilities! I am here to pull the carpet from beneath all your constructed points of view. Every time I do that there is a possibility that you may become more aware, and hence I become more aware, and everyone around you becomes more aware. How does it get any better than that?

What if you have the ability to pick up thoughts and feelings of other people? What if I was to tell you that you are a walking antenna. Have you ever woken up on a Monday morning and felt like it is the end of the universe? All you want to do is stay in bed and not face the world. You love your job but you just don't want to play. You start thinking about all the reasons why you should not work? Or have you walked into a room where people have been arguing and you could cut the tension with a knife? Are they your thoughts and feelings? Who do they belong to? What if you were just picking up all the thoughts and feelings of everyone around you? Would you like to return those to sender, please? This is one of those talents and abilities that you have as a humanoid. Yep, that's right you are not human. You look human. People think you are human, but you are actually humanoid. You are more like the Triple J three-armed drummer than you think. Here is a wedgie (a wedgie is something that takes you by surprise, it wedges a door open). Your whole life you have believed that you are human. You spend your time trying to fit in, when you know you just don't. That takes a hell of a lot of energy. Have you ever thought that you don't fit in because there is something wrong with you? Or have you had that fantasy when you were a kid that you were actually the subject of an alien experiment, that this reality was not real. Or that you must be adopted? Or all of the above? This may sound weird but those fantasies are probably closer to truth than you think. What if it was an awareness that you were unwilling to receive because if you lived your truth you would be persecuted for it? You learned at a very early age to shut up when you started to talk about your reality, because most of the people around you would chastise you in some way or judge you as weird. So you locked the real you away and now you have come to believe that you are human.

Humans will judge everything, Humanoids will judge themselves. Humans like the status quo, Humanoids like change. Humans are very methodical, Humanoids are likely to jump from one project to another. Humans see everything as black and white, Humanoids see infinite possibilities. Neither is better than the other, they are just different. But when a Humanoid spends his life trying to be Human, something that they are not, they use enormous amounts of energy to hold that mask in place. When a Humanoid is acting like a Human, they become miserable, they suffer and they can get sick.

Isn't that great to know that you have actually been pretending to be something you aren't? Now that you can recognise this you can start to claim all those parts of you that you have hidden and start to become whole again, start to heal. Would you be willing to acknowledge that you're different from many humans out there?

A Human will judge this concept of Human / Humanoid. A Humanoid may resist to start with and then feel relief to know that they are not in fact wrong, they are just different. By the way, a Human will judge someone for being too sleepy, they will call them a lazy asshole, (maybe not to their face), but that doesn't matter because a Humanoid can actually pick that thought up, and you know what most Humanoids do with a thought like that, they think it is their own, they will judge themselves, they will store this in the body, they will work harder and harder to justify this point of view and prove that it is not real (because it's not), and work themselves into an early grave. That was my experience (and it is no longer true for me). So everything that that just brought up would you be willing to destroy and uncreate it? Yabba Dabba Doooooo!

Hey look behind you now, it's that famous Russian Philosopher, Justin IPOV. It is just an interesting point of view. Use the tools Luke, use the tools!

Tools and Tips
- It is not "better" to be Human or Humanoid, they are just different.
- Knowing the difference means you can respond in different ways making life easier for everyone.
- Knowing you are Humanoid allows you to know why you judge the hell out of yourself.
- Being Humanoid means you are very, very, very psychic and hence you think all the thoughts and feeling you have are yours. They are not!
- When you acknowledge you are Humanoid, you will start to bring back all those little bits that you have cut off and start to become whole.

Chapter 8

Judgement

Hard work pays off in the future. Laziness pays off now.

The thing about judgement is that we have bought the idea that everything fits into good or bad, positive or negative, black or white, right or wrong. That everything has a charge, a polarity (this is a very Human concept). When you choose to live in polarities you are not choosing awareness. So let us say the tax office has lost your address and they can't find you to pay you back $5000. Six months later you are making some enquiries about another tax issue, they bring you up on their computer and tell you they owe you five grand (true story!). Immediately you will judge this as a good thing. You have just put the brakes on for anything greater showing up. Ouch! Stay in the question and you could ask, "How does it get any better than that?" You just get your colonoscopy results back and it shows you have chronic pandemic ulceration. You immediately go into, "This is a bad thing", by doing this you immediately go to the wrongness of your body and you stop anything greater showing up. Double ouch! So stay in the question and you could ask, "How can it get any better than that?" In the early stages when practising this it will probably sound more like, "Put on a brave face. Okay, f***, okay. Oh! How does it get any better? Uh, no, what was it. Ah, yes! How does it get any better than that? Yeah, that's it! Yeah, how can it get any better than that?" Then you may look the surgeon in the eye (whose job it is to sell you surgery - that's his point of view) and say, "Okay, so what else is possible?" or "That's an interesting point of view." You haven't judged anything or anyone. You haven't resisted and reacted to the news and put your body into fight / flight, into stress. You haven't aligned and agreed and bought a point of view (a very expensive one). What have you done? By this time you have asked half a dozen questions and the universe is already at work for you. How does it get any better than that? This tells the universe that you are aware that some changes may be necessary. Sounds rough, but what's the alternative? You could go into a spiral of emotion, of pain and suffering and hence more disease. What would you like to choose, disease or awareness?

By the way, the universe sees no difference between manifesting $1 or a million bucks, a diseased body part or a well functioning body part. It also does not comprehend fast or slow. Consciousness has no point of view. It judges nothing and includes everything. It is just waiting for you to ask a question and deliver to you what you would like. If you keep focusing on pain, suffering and gory, guess what you get? If you start to ask more questions, different questions, more expansive questions, guess what you get? These are all limitations from judgements, all limitations from the Human constructed reality. Wherever you judge something you are compiling evidence that your belief is right. Are you willing to give up the rightness of your disease, all the significance that you have given it and all those judgements that hold your disease in place? Would you be willing to destroy and uncreate all that utterly, butterly? (A little tongue in cheek for our UK readers!) "Yippee!" That's your body saying that!

As a Humanoid you are constantly in judgement about yourself. Something is not as it should be and you go to the wrongness of you. "I am so stupid for causing this. It is all my fault that this situation is the way it is!" Judgement upon judgement upon judgement upon judgement. So, every time you make a judgement about yourself you are saying, "I am wrong. My body is wrong because of disease, because it can't run a 4 minute mile, because it is too fat, too thin, too tall…" Is it no wonder that your body is so ill? What can we do here? What tool is available to help us destroy those judgements? I assume that if you are still reading this you are interested in change, so I'm going to throw in some more wacky stuff here. The only time you can make a judgement is when you have done that or been that. Sit with that for a while. It is so liberating. I hear you say, "But I haven't been a criminal in this life or a back stabber or …." In this life maybe not, but what about other lives? Was that a sneaky little 'but' there? It's a cute butt, but not required! What about all the TV programs you have watched and picked up all the judgements from there, from everyone else? Here is the wacky bit, every time you have a judgement, **POD and POC when I was that or did that**.

"What?" Top of the class for asking a question! Have you noticed that when you ask a question, the next chapter or something in your life, shows you a possibility. Sometimes, it is immediate, sometimes it appears to take a little longer.

When I first heard this my mind went "ugh." I have since found out that that is so cool. Every time my mind does that "ugh" thing I know there is an opportunity for me to change, to become aware, that I am willing to receive a possibility. The first time I heard this idea of when you have a judgement you have to have been or done that, so POD and POC it, I was having my first 'Bars' session. I was at the end of my tether, so to speak, and I just didn't care what it meant, I was just so willing to try anything. I was staying with a Human and a Humanoid-desperately-seeking Human, so there were a lot of judgements flying around. I used it for 3 weeks with as many judgements as possible. One night (with my new-found body) I was preparing to go for a walk at about 9.00 pm. My Human friend said, "Be careful. It is unsafe to walk the streets at this time." Judgement! Judgement! Judgement alert! POD and POC when I was that or did that? Pow! Something changed! I realised I was buying into it. That 'it' wasn't part of my reality. I was suddenly aware that I had asked my body and my body wouldn't put me in danger. I remembered that 3 weeks previously I couldn't even have contemplated a walk at 9.00pm as I had been a waif. So, remember, for any judgement, POD and POC when I was or did that.

My mate POC means point of creation, and my other mate POD means point of destruction! Very simply, by PODDING and POCCING something we go to the point where we bought that point of view and destroy it. It no longer clutters up our reality and it allows us to choose something different. We can choose in the 'now' and not from December 25, 1967 when I bought the lie that Santa was real!!!

Would you be willing to destroy and uncreate all the judgements you have bought? That would be a real miracle, not your body healing, that is the effect. My editor, Cas, asked me "What does this mean?" Good question. Living in the question without judgement is a miracle, it is being conscious. When this occurs the body does not have to put up with all the lies that you have told it to be. This allows the right body for you to show up. Hence healing is the effect of the miracle. Wow, what a significant point of view. Lets destroy and uncreate any significance around that. What else is possible?

How do you know if it is a judgement or an observation? Wherever you have misidentified an observation as a judgement, are you willing to destroy and uncreate that? When it is a judgement there is usually some charge to it or a justification. An observation that someone is a "con-man" is okay, it as an awareness and then you can choose whether to do business with them or not. If you say that person is a "f***** big asshole and should learn to drive properly" that is a judgement. Can you sense the difference in energy between the two? The second one is a judgement, and at sometime you too have made some crazy choices at the traffic lights! So POD and POC when I was that or did that. It is much easier on your body than justifying the rightness of your point of view and locking that judgement into your body.

Tools and Tips
- For you to make a judgement of someone you have to have been or done that in order to judge so…
- For any judgement POD and POC when I was or did that.
- Stop judging yourself. You are nowhere near as stuffed up as you think you are!
- If you made it this far, here is a question you can ask, don't look for answer, feel the energy of it "What is it that you love about this disease?" Keep asking until the energy shifts.

Chapter 9

What would it be like to live without a story?

A day without sunshine is like night.

What if I told you everything was a lie. Pretty outrageous statement. This realisation was so liberating. Being able to receive this meant that I no longer had to believe anything, no need to buy into anyone's point of view. I no longer had to waste all that energy on believing or trying to fit in. So much of my teens through to my early forties was trying to fit in by buying everybody else's beliefs. I recall actually thinking to myself, "I am envious of these people that they have such a belief, life must be so easy for them." Whoa, what a head trip! What I didn't realise then was that if I could be myself, I wouldn't need to buy these lies as real to fit in. Where have you bought lies to make yourself fit into somebody else's reality, and are you willing to destroy and uncreate all those? Would you like to be you? Have you got any idea what that would look like? If your answer is "no", that is cool. If you are an infinite being would you be able to categorise yourself into an idea?

As mentioned earlier Gary suggests that 98% of what we think and feel is not ours. That's why when a thought or feeling comes up we ask the question, "Who does this belong to?" It often lightens up and moves on.

Every thought or feeling is like a computer program that we have bought and installed or implanted in us. We have bought this as real because it served some sort of function at the time, i.e. to fit into a group (family, cultural, peer...) or get a need met. We then work from these programs or points of view as being real all the time, and we make our choices from these programs, these lies. They no longer serve the function that we chose them for, so they are now outdated. Would you be willing to choose something different?

To use a computer analogy, it's like buying a top-of-the-range computer in 1997, a Pentium 1 with 3GB of memory (I won't even mention the old ZX80 that was my first computer!) and trying to use this with Vista, MP3, Internet etc. in 2007. It just does not work. Imagine, (no, destroy that) look at the programs you bought when you were ten years old. Are you still using those programs to deal with your life now? Is that insane? Yes it is. And that is exactly what you have done. It is okay, you are not unique in this everyone does it. Wherever you have tried to prove that you are unique or special, would you like to destroy and uncreate that and just be you?

So...would you like to pull the plug on the Pentium 1 and upgrade to consciousness now? Please don't misinterpret this and update to a top of the range Intel duo180GB laptop with Vista. Because in 10 years that hardware and programs will be out-of-date and you'll be operating from the past again. What would it be like to completely wipe all programs off your hard drive and operate from knowing, not from thought or feeling? Would you be willing to do that? Have you noticed that as soon as you have bought a new computer it is outdated? Well, consciousness is even faster. As soon as you align and agree or resist and react to a point of view, you have bought it and immediately it is out-of-date and we have done this with everything. Is it no wonder you have a disease? All the tools presented here will help you destroy these lies you have chosen and allow you to live a life of ease, joy and glory.

We use oodles of energy defending these lies and justifying why we chose them. We also spend huge amounts of time and energy judging other's points of view because they don't agree and align with ours. We expend large amounts of energy judging ourselves: I'm stupid, I'm too skinny, I'm too fat, I'm not good enough…(and they don't have to be negative judgements either). The point of view that I was too skinny for example, was one that ran for me 24/7. This lie, this judgement or someone else's point of view that I bought, created my body, helped shape it and ultimately started to destroy it. And it is not just the point of view about our bodies that destroys it, it is every judgement, every good, bad and ugly one. The more we think them, feel them, say them, act them out, the stronger they become, the more concrete, the more solid. (Or as we say in Access they become fixed points of view).

I have a friend who has arthritis which he takes medication for. I recently stayed with him for 3 months. I can see that all those fixed points of view that he believes are real and his unwillingness to change, has created this disease. It is like not greasing the ball joints on your car because you have the point of view that it costs too much. What happens? They seize up. Because there is a part of you that sees the insanity of this, you dig your heels in and you justify your point of view, creating more solidity. Most people would rather defend their point of view than change it. Does this friend take his medication to ease the pain or so he can keep his points of view?

That disease you have created is a result of all the fixed points of view you have locked into your body. Would you like to destroy and uncreate all those and have the vulnerability to admit that you are stubborn and resist change? Grateful sighs expressed by body! The good news is that I have witnessed people change on a dime. One minute they have a point of view that they are unwilling to change with a body that is tight and inflexible, the next they are a million years younger with tons of energy. Sometimes it appears to take a little longer.

Are you the type of person, or do you know someone that may try these methods just to prove them wrong, just to prove that their point of view is right? And it will happen. I work with people that understand this stuff during a session but a week later they are choosing the same crap! They justify it by saying that the tools don't work. When I ask them if they are using the tools there is usually a brief period of silence before they rush on to their next story. Is that sane? Interesting point of view!

What are some of the lies you have bought about your body? Too fat, too thin, too short, too ugly, penis too small, breasts too small, breasts to big…? Once you are vulnerable enough to admit that you have these points of view, you will have the possibility to change them. You don't need to write a book to admit these or shout them out, or call your local news station, just to yourself is enough. Are you willing to give up all these points of view and judgements about your body? Will you claim, own and acknowledge that you are the creator of your disease? Are you willing to destroy and uncreate all those points of view and judgements you have about your body?

Somewhere along the line someone said to me, "Hey, you're too skinny!" And I bought it, whether it was true or not. Every time someone made a comment on the thinness of my body I used this to prove the point of view that I bought (I had an investment in it now). Really, it was just someone else's point of view that I chose to buy, and was that a costly transaction! I paid for that one for at least 40 years. It was like a never ending flexi-rent. The good news is it is not mine, and the great news about flexi-rent is that at the end of the term, although you have paid at least twice the amount of the original price, you get the choice to continue or give it back. The insanity of it is that most people continue to stay with their commitment to flexi-rent, so they can prove that the money they have spent and the decisions that they made, were right. Would you like to give up flexi-renting your life now?

Recently there were three of us slim blokes standing in a shop. I recognised a new energy. I suddenly realised I was not judging myself as skinny. Instead I sensed a vibration of vitality, of energy. This took 7 months of using these tools presented here. I no longer judge my body, I now commune with it. I am grateful for it. Has my health improved? You bet!

You choose to buy these lies and then base many choices on them. To continue the skinny program for example, I made choices like, "I can't get laid because I'm too skinny, I have to eat more because I'm too skinny." I spent a lot of energy fighting it too. I would get angry when someone said, "You need to put some meat on your bones," and then I would spend more time and energy justifying the anger. It became another story, another reason not to show up as me. It was also very painful for my body. As Dain says, "Stop judging your body." So what will it take to enjoy your body as it is? Can you find parts of your body that are not wrong, that you like?

When someone tries to sell you their point of view, whether it's a family member, a car salesman, a newsman, or a politician, you could say aloud or in your head "Interesting point of view." You can use it with your own story, thoughts and feelings, "Interesting point of view I had that point of view." Gary suggests using this for <u>every</u> point of view you have for twelve months. Double dog dare you!

By using the tool "interesting point of view" you free yourself from all the lies that you have chosen to buy into. You are actually being aware that these thoughts and feelings are just lies. If that is too hard for you to receive at this moment, is that somebody else's point of view? It breaks the loop. It starts allowing you to make choices from consciousness instead of automatically making a choice based on outdated programmes. Whenever, wherever you have bought a point of view, are you willing to destroy and uncreate that?

The last part of the previous paragraph is a simple clearing statement. Clearings are powerful tools used in Access. I used to keep a journal. In that journal I saw a pattern of thoughts and feelings coming up. Sometimes it was just going deeper, but many kept coming back even though I thought I had let them go. It wasn't until Access came along that I realized I wasn't clearing them. They had some sort of glue that allowed them to keep coming back. The vestment in these points of view, judgments and the story and the decisions that I had made, kept them bound to me. I was trapped in a vicious cycle and my symptoms appeared to flare accordingly.

Once I started clearing I started healing. Could clearing instigate healing? I just got that as I was writing it, I feel lighter, so it is true for me. If it gets lighter it's true for you, if it gets heavier it is a lie for you. Oh yeah, and that can change in any ten seconds. When you follow the energy there is no need to make anything concrete, that, my friend, creates a limitation.

Are you getting angry or defensive while you are reading this? Are you operating from some sort of old program that is inhibiting your ability to receive? What I am presenting here is an interesting point of view. If you use these tools you will receive what your body requires from this book, to help facilitate your own healing. If you stay in anger and defence, fight and flight, and over working your autonomic nervous system, you're not going to receive what your body requires and you may continue to use huge amounts of energy fighting, resisting and reacting. Could this energy be channelled towards healing? The choice is yours, it always is.

What are you unwilling to receive that if you could receive it would allow you to stop resisting and reacting or aligning and agreeing with every point of view you have regarding your body?

Tools and Tips
- 98 % of thoughts, feelings and emotions are not yours.
- Please do not feel the need to justify anything, a "because" is a pretty good indication your are justifying. If it is light for you it is true for you (at least for that 10 seconds).
- If it is heavy for you, it is not true for you, ask more questions.
- You always have choice.
- To learn more about clearings, you can contact a facilitator at www.accessconsciosness.com

Chapter 10

Sex and the nervous system

What happens if you get scared half to death, twice?

Your body enjoys being sexy and sensual. It loves being touched and it loves touching in nurturing and caring ways. Sex is not copulation but it can include that. Sex is energy and can be encountered with any body, including sex and sensuality with your self. Sex is receiving and gifting at the same time. Let's get one thing straight, sex is energy. It is not copulation, fucking, force or violence. It is fun and sensual.

If you have a point of view that sex is fighting, getting your rocks off or is painful and disgusting, then that's not sex, that's violence, force and power over others. If this is your point of view about sex, then you are using huge quantities of energy avoiding sex, or doing violent sex, and putting your nervous system under great stress from avoiding or performing, and this will cause more suffering, pain, gory and sickness.

Interesting point of view! To write this book I used a speech-to-text program because I was not very fast at typing and this program recognised fighting as "fuck king." Are you aware of the acronym F.U.C.K, what it actually means? It means "fornication under consent of the King." It meant that the knights and nobility could take anyone and copulate with them. Is that sort of "sex" nurturing?

Here is another point of view. A little boy comes running in to the farm house and says out loud, "Fuck!" His Mom is shocked and asks her son, "Do you know what that word means?" "Yes mommy, it means the electric fence is on!"

If you have one of these points of view would you like to change it and release all that energy to help you heal? Would you like caring, nurturing, healing sex and sensuality?

Firstly, one of the basic things about sex is you don't need anyone to be sexy or sensual with. You can practice by yourself. How does it get any better than that? Wherever, whenever you bought the idea that you require a partner or a soul mate, to have great sex with, would you be willing to destroy and uncreate all that?

Secondly, nature is an incredible sexual dynamo. Taking a walk in a forest or, if you are unable to walk, sitting on the beach, is a great way to receive sexual energy, to receive orgasmic energy. I often sing when I walk on the beach or in a forest. I touch the trees, I feel the sand between my toes. My singing and touching is gratitude, it is a response to the gift I am receiving and thus becomes a gift to nature, which is always willing to receive. Recently I had a full body orgasm on Fraser Island just by doing this, there was no ejaculation, no touching of the genitals, just that intense orgasmic feeling and it lasted a lot longer than orgasm through copulation or masturbation. That same week my body changed again and symptoms dramatically reduced. How does it get any better than that? And what else is possible? And what would it be like to live in that orgasmic state all the time?

That same week I met a woman who was totally vulnerable with me, and I was totally willing to receive from her (usually as a man I had bought the point of view that I had to be the giver). Whilst at a dinner party she touched my legs, hugged me, stroked my body and flirted with me. We shared a meal, we danced. It was so much fun, and at the end of the party we hugged and never saw each other again. That is sex. That is sensuality. And you know what? The diarrhoea I had stopped that night. Interesting point of view!

Thirdly, if you have hang-ups about sex they could be contributing to your disease. What if you were willing to clear these hang-ups about sex? How much potency are you avoiding or refusing with regards to sex?

Oh, if you have any resistance to this chapter you have a hang-up about sex. A word of awareness here, this chapter is only going to get more intense from here on.

What would it take to receive nurturing and caring sex for your body? Would it be possible to ask your body whom it would like sex with? Who to be sensual with? Who to copulate with?

These are all great questions to ask to start clearing hang-ups about sex and sexual energy. Gary and Dain have put together a beautiful book on sex and relationships called, "Sex is not a four letter word but relationship oftentimes is," and I would thoroughly recommend reading this book several times, in order to gain new insights into sex.

Vulnerability is not being a doormat, or being submissive. For me it is the ability to be honest with myself, and in that honesty I can totally drop all the energy I had been using to hide or defend my point of view regarding sex, or anything else, and have all that energy available to me for my body to heal.

I will be vulnerable right now. I will talk about my sex life. Part of this vulnerability is not caring what others may think. "Hey, this is me and if your point of view is that I'm weird, I don't care. If your point of view is pity, then that is your point of view and I am not buying it today."

So here goes. I used to masturbate a lot, usually with the aide of pornography. Masturbating had become a way of releasing tension and was quick, tiring and ugly. It was also used to repress the feelings of anxiety, doom and gloom that I had bought and thought were mine. I didn't know how to ask to be touched or how to touch. Ejaculation was the goal so I could release pent up energy. It was force and violence against myself and often my partner, and usually pretty quick. At one stage when I was sick I threw all the pornography out. I felt light when I chose this and my body went into remission. For this reason I swung to the other side and repressed all sex. I chose celibacy. I became sick again and to release all that repressed energy I swung again to forceful masturbation. This put extreme stress on my sympathetic nervous system. I was constantly activating the flight/fight response and putting my body under extreme duress. On top of that I felt disgusted by this. I thought of myself as perverted. I had bought a lot of other people's points of view about sex. There appeared to be no-one to talk to about this and that's because 99.999999% of the population have some hang-up about sex, a polarized point of view about sex. It's probably the most taboo subject on the planet and everyone has a point of view about it.

There was a monk who was a scribe. He was copying a document when he came across a passage that was very smudged. He was very proud of his work and he liked to be accurate, so he decided to check out the original manuscript. Off to the library he went. It was a very old document so he had to be admitted to the inner sanctum where all the originals were kept. He opened the original book and found the passage. He read it once, could not believe it, read it twice, and then a third time. Then he cried out in despair. The monks outside the inner sanctum were stunned out of their silence. They rushed in to find out what was wrong with their brother. "What is wrong?" they asked when they saw their brother weeping over the open book. Through sobs and sniffles the monk replied, "the word is celebrate not celibate!" How many points of view have you bought about sex that are not true? Would you be willing to destroy and uncreate all those?

So, I had created a point of view that I was killing myself with sex. Not a very nurturing point of view for a body already under stress! So I started to ask some questions, for example, what would it take to find out the truth about sex?

The answer came in the form of two men called Gary and Dain. Their vulnerability in sharing their knowing and experience about sex, has helped me clear up a lot about what I thought were my hang ups and were actually points of view that I had bought. Now I can walk into a party full of strangers and be sexy. How does it get any better than that?

You can have lots of sex and sensuality if your body requires it. Lots of caring and nurturing sex with yourself or with a partner that your body enjoys. This means you can start to have sex from the parasympathetic nervous system. When this system is activated, it creates relaxation in the body. Touch yourself, caress, relax, ask to be touched how YOU like to be touched. If it's not what you like, choose something else. Please don't put someone else first. This will destroy your body.

A nun, badly needing to use the restroom, walked into a local club. The place was hopping with music and loud conversation, and every once in a while the lights would turn off. Each time the lights would go out, the place would erupt into cheers. However, when the party goers saw the nun, the room went dead silent. She walked up to the bartender, and asked, "May I please use the restroom?" The bartender replied, "OK, but I should warn you that there is a statue of a naked man in there wearing only a fig leaf."

"Well, in that case I'll just look the other way." said the nun.

So the bartender showed the nun to the back of the restaurant. After a few minutes, she came back out, and the whole place stopped just long enough to give the nun a loud round of applause. She went to the bartender and said, "Sir, I don't understand. Why did they applaud me just because I went to the restroom?"

"Well, now they know you're one of us," said the bartender.

"But, I still don't understand," said the puzzled nun.

"You see," laughed the bartender, "every time someone lifts the fig leaf on that statue, the lights go out."

Sex is not serious, if it is you ain't doing sex.

Tools and Tips
- Sex is not just copulation or ejaculation.
- Sex and sensuality is nurturing for your body.
- Ask your body how it would like to be pampered. Mine likes me to tickle it, and to have regular manicures.
- If your body desires it, have lots of sex and sensuality by yourself or with a partner.
- Ask your body what clothes it feels sexy in.
- Ask questions of your partner.
- If you don't like what your partner is doing, ask them to change it.
- Ask your body if it would like sex and with whom.
- If sex is forceful you are not doing your body any favours.
- Sex is fun.
- Take time for sex.
- When you feel yourself starting to contract, slow down, relax and allow the energy to expand.
- Take time out in nature. Nature gifts of itself with no expectation.

Chapter 11

Hidden talents and abilities

Why do psychics have to ask you for your name?

I have the incredible talent and ability to take on someone else's thoughts, feelings and emotions and as a psychic I used this ability quite often. No big deal! It came to me quite easily. What I didn't recognise was that I could and did store other's insane thoughts, feelings and emotions in my body. Would an infinite being take on all the pain and suffering of someone else? When asking this question it became known to me that I had what I call a "Jesus complex." Interesting point of view! For whatever reason, somewhere I bought into the point of view that by taking on their pain and suffering I could heal them. My mother often said to me when I was sick or hurt, "If I could take on your pain I would." As a kid I wondered how that could be possible and created that in my life. It is that simple. In some ten seconds of unconsciousness we can wonder what it would be like, have a thought and 'POW', that desire is picked up by the universe. The universe doesn't discriminate when it comes to manifesting what you ask for. Sometimes it shows up immediately, sometimes in 20 years. Does taking on someone's pain or suffering from them aide them? In trying to do this, is it taking their choice away to be sick? Once when asking the question, "Who does this belong to?" I recognised that I used to take on my ex-wife's period pain. Interesting point of view! The disease I chose even mimicked some of the symptoms, for example: cyclic in nature, bleeding, cramping and emotional. Am I describing ulcerative colitis or menstruation? Did this help my wife's pain? Did it actually add to her stress? You bet. Not a very kind thing to do.

How much of your disease is actually you taking on somebody else's pain and suffering? If you do this, has this helped the person long-term? Would an infinite being truly choose this? Would you choose to put somebody else's pain and suffering before you? Is this raising your consciousness or the consciousness of the other? Or does it create more pain and suffering? Who are you to think you have the right to take somebody else's pain and suffering away? Have they not chosen it? If someone asks you for help or you offer and they truly take that offer, you can ask them questions, you can use all the techniques you know, you can allow them their point of view and through questions you can help open doors for them, and then they can choose to go through or not. As soon as you try to take anything from them or push your point of view down their throats for whatever reason, you have just shot yourself in the foot. Are you willing to destroy and uncreate saving the universe and putting yourself second?

Tools and Tips
- How much pain are you taking on for others?
- Don't buy the story as real, as soon as you wonder what it would be like, you have bought it. Ouch!
- Acknowledge your talents and abilities and then you can choose to use them. Or not. Don't, and you will be a victim and that is also a choice.

Chapter 12
Expansion

Are you inside your body or is your body inside you? Have you bought religious, spiritual or human beliefs that the body is a useless pile of debris and needs to be transcended or that your body is "it" and once "it" is gone, life is gone?

What if we chose embodiment to have fun? What if life wasn't about learning a lesson, or transcending anything?

When our body hurts, when we are in pain, when we are suffering, emotionally, mentally or physically, we focus all the energy we have on that pain and suffering. We bought this point of view. I fell over as a kid on the way to infant school, which is not where I wanted to go. Mummy was there, my knee was bleeding. I started crying. I ran into mummy's arms, and she soothed me in the way that only mummies can. I was manipulating mummy. Both my attention and mummy's attention was on the pain and suffering of my knee, and I had a huge investment in the grazed knee, that is not wanting to go to school, so more energy went to the wound, which created more pain. I still have the scar 37 years later. What happened here was that the focus went to the pain, I contracted, I made myself smaller in order to get what I wanted, I hurt my knee. This point of view locked itself into the cells of my knee. And the more I learned to get what I wanted, the more I cut off my true self, the more I contracted. What would it be like when we are in pain or misery if we expanded?

Would you like to try? Take an example from your own life, where you have felt bad about someone you really care for. Maybe you were angry. Close your eyes and recall how that felt, now start to expand your energy. Expand it out past your body, fill the room out to the edges of the house, the street, the town you are in. Expand out to your country, your region, the whole planet. Expand out to the moon, the sun, the whole solar system. Expand past the galaxy, to infinity. Has that bad feeling, that anger, disappointment, whatever, gotten bigger or has it dissipated? Dissipated right? So what if you were to do that when your body is in pain. Instead of contracting, expand. The pain may still be there, but it will no longer be significant. Well done you!

As I am writing this I am perceiving more symptoms, and my mind is becoming concerned. There are thoughts of doubt in my body's abilities. I make more story. I make every gurgle, every fart, every runny shit and every tiny speck of blood significant. I can remember my then father-in-law, who I admired greatly, saying that bleeding was serious and I should get it checked out. I bought this lock, stock and barrel and made the bleeding significant, important and serious. The more I weaved my story, the more bleeding occurred. Now, when this happens I am able to clear it. Back when I was in the story big time, the story of the disease ran my life. Everything I was doing was to rid myself of the disease and thus I created more story, instead of making a communion with my body and coming from the energy and space of consciousness. I am creating my life the way I like it to be. I am so grateful that Access came into my life.

So, where to now? What will it take to heal? Keep asking questions. The power is in the question. Ask your body what it would like to wear, with whom it would like to have sex, what medication it requires…destroy and uncreate anywhere you bought the story and ask questions. What will it take to heal? Demand it! Whatever it will take to heal I am willing to do. Who does this belong to? Where does this come from? Keep asking, keep sending it back to sender. How long do I keep asking? As long as it takes…20 minutes, 2 hours, three days. "Who does this belong to? Where does it come from? Return to sender with all the consciousness of the universe attached to it." Every thought and every emotion and every perceived pain, "Who does this belong to? Where does this come from? And return to sender with all the consciousness of the universe attached to it. What is right about this that I am not getting? What is it I love about this?"

How did I create this? Do we create all that is wonderful and exciting in our lives? Are we willing to say, "Gee, I created all that wealth in my life?" Yes! So who creates all the pain and suffering? Could that also be us? I literally created all the shit in my life and it only takes ten seconds of unconscious thought to get the ball rolling, and that point of view that was bought could have been in the last minute, last week, last year, 40 years ago. How often have you bought that can of baked beans and put it in your cupboard and forgotten it was there until you move? And you don't even like baked beans. Could it be the same for buying all the shit and disease in our lives? In some ten seconds of unconsciousness you wonder what it would be like to have cancer? Wham! Your body hears it, the universe hears it. You hear your grandmother on the phone to your mum and she says, "I have been diagnosed with diverticulitis"* and as a kid you say, "I wonder what that is? I wonder what that would be like to have?" And then Granny explains the symptoms and you have just bought the disease by wondering what that would be like. Ouch!

"Too difficult!" I hear you say, so, "Who does that thought belong to?" "That sounds crazy," (and creating disease is totally sane?) "Who does that belong to?" "I can't do that because…" "Who does that belong to?" "But I'm special" ("get over it" as Gary would say.) "Who does that belong to?" "But you don't understand, my disease is different." (And nor would I choose to understand your disease, in trying to understand I buy your point of view.) "Who does that belong to?" "Who does that belong to?" "Who does that belong to?" "Who does that belong to?" Are you willing to make the changes necessary for your body to heal? "No?" Come back when you are ready. Put this book down and when you have spent all your money, when your health is really terrible, when your body is close to death, then you can pick up the book again. For what reason would you choose the last option? Would it not be easier just to do whatever it takes now while you still have the energy? I did all that, and I can tell you, you don't have to. I am writing this book from consciousness, I am writing it so you can be more aware. You don't have to create disease to become aware, just skip that bit and become aware. There are people waiting for you to be who you really are. We would like more aware people to play with. Or not! The choice is yours.

Are you looking for the answer in these questions? Stop. What will it take to ask questions with genuine wonder?

Tools and Tips
- Stop looking for the answer. There is no need to find one and when you do, it stops the energy flow. Instead, be aware of the energy, if it is light, or lightens up, it is true for you.
- Ask questions.
- Who does this belong to?
- Where did that pain come from?
- How did I create this?
- It is a good idea to focus on the pain, really get into it. **NOT!**

*Diverticulitis is a form of bowel disease

Chapter 13
Access Diet

Life isn't like a box of chocolates, it's more like a jar of jalapenos. What you do today, might burn your butt tomorrow.

Have you ever looked at the word diet? The root of this word is "die." Every time you use this word you're asking to "die." I know this from experience. In the early stages of dis-ease I was hospitalised twice. The second time I was a few hours from death. (I am very grateful to all those doctors, friends and therapists during that time). I had a belief about diet that food was the cornerstone of my disease, that food was a possible cause of the dis-ease and hence I was refusing anything that didn't match this point of view. Disease and "die"t, I almost did.

What would it be like if we allowed our body to choose what was best for it? All the ideas and beliefs you have around dieting and the word 'diet' would you please destroy and uncreate all those? All the ideas and beliefs you have around any specific foods (eg. chocolate is bad, coffee is bad, vegies are healthy…) would you please destroy and uncreate all those?

Now that we have cleared that, it is possible to be willing to receive what it is that your body requires regarding nutrition. What will it take for your body to digest the appropriate foods that it requires? You can ask this question of your own body. You may find that what comes is something new, something you've never thought about. It could be a book or a person or a dog or a TV programme that leads you to the next step. So, here are a few things about receiving your body's wisdom. Firstly, you can use the 'ask your body technique' about everything that involves your body. Secondly, the body requires 3 things from food to function: sugar, salt and water, especially when you are clearing a lot of judgements, points of view etc. Just reading this book may start to unlock the limitations that you have. When we start to unlock them the brain goes through some changes and requires more salt, sugar, water and sleep. How does it get any better than that?

There are many different types of sugar, for example, sucrose (processed sugar), glucose and fructose which are simple sugars and may take very little to digest. Other sugars like dextrose, have more bonds between the molecules and may require more digestion, as do polysaccharides, which are complex carbohydrates.

Salt is a general term for minerals which can be found in fruits, vegies, meat etc. It is not restricted to table salt and also includes sea salt and rock salt.

Water is an important component of any diet. There are lots of different types of water, some are cleaner, some are more acidic, others more alkaline.

An Interesting point of view about water that has come to light within the last few years is its ability to take on a vibration of the energy projected at it. What if we have a lot of judgements about water, would that affect the quality of the water we drink? One global company that bottles water called "Good Vibes for you," takes this into account, just the name of the company suggests that water will have vibrations that are beneficial for you. How does it get any better than that?

Okay, so enough of the technical stuff, you can find that anywhere. Sometimes it is just so easy to buy all this "diet stuff" as real. Notice how heavy all this information about food is? I even used the word "important" when talking about water, now that is heavy. Anywhere we emphasis anything, give it importance or significance, that is usually where we have a fixed point of view. So, lets destroy and uncreate all that. How many points of view have you bought about diet, including the ones above, that limit your bodies ability to function? Would you be willing to destroy all those and allow your body to choose?

If you are what I used to be like, and have done lots of research in this area, it can be very confusing. To cut this confusion from your menu, you can ask your body. What a novel idea! Sugar is for energy, water is necessary to transport all this and for appropriate cell function along with the salts. If unsure ask your body. You may not believe this whilst your body is in pain, but your body is a remarkable being and can cope with most things. Does your body want to live? I know that it will say, "Yeah!" That's what it was born for, to live, to move, to dance, to have sex and fun. All the dis-ease, pain and suffering in your body is a result of the beliefs and judgements that you have bought. Will you claim, own and acknowledge that you have created this pain and suffering? Wow! What a creator! So, it's not working for you now - choose something different! Are you willing to receive what you have been unwilling to receive from your body? What a great gift. What if pain was just an intensity of feeling?

Back to diet, oops, body nutrition! Could the root of the word 'nutrition' mean 'to nurture?' Here are some tools to eat with awareness:

Tools and Tips
- Ask your body.
- Ask your body.
- Ask your body.
- Use "Body would you like to digest this?" It has a very different meaning to "Body would you like this?"
- Here is an interesting question for you. Does your body need to eat the food or take the vitamin to get what it requires from it? Could you just ask your body to pull what it requires from the item?
- Taste the first bite of each food with awareness. Smell it, feel the temperature, the texture…
- When it starts to taste like cardboard, your body has had enough.
- Get out of the habit that breakfast means that you eat a certain type of food, or lunch has to be at a certain time. If your body wants chocolate for breakfast, then okay. If it doesn't feel light ask a question like, "Okay body, would you like to digest this? Would you like something sugary? Can you get what you would like from something else…?"
- Ask lots of questions.
- Ask "Who does this belong to?" Perhaps the craving is not yours.
- When in a shop, a restaurant, around others, you can always put a little bubble around you when choosing food. Just ask "bubble." This would be the only time I would recommend cutting your receiving off from the universe.

- <u>If you have any point of view around a particular food you can destroy and uncreate it and pod and poc it before asking your body if it wants to eat it. (just say those words "I destroy and uncreate" or "Pod and Poc any points of view I have about this orange…"</u>
- Finally, shops, food and sales people all have their own consciousness, they want to be eaten or sell you something. So be aware, are you consuming a food for yourself, for something or someone else?

Chapter 14
Energy Work

Just remember -- if the world didn't suck, we would all fall off.

This chapter describes several techniques that you can use easily with your body. There are no hard and fast rules, just follow and direct the energy. If you have used other techniques and find that they are no longer working for you, you may find these helpful. All the methods, means or modalities and other techniques that stop you from playing with the energy, for example visualisation, saying a special mantra while standing on your head, or any other points of views that you have bought and no longer work for you, would you be willing to destroy and uncreate these?

Did you know we all have the ability to direct energy? We can suck energy through us like we suck a milkshake through a curly whirly straw (do you remember those?), and we can push or flow energy like water shooting through a hose. The classic car salesman is a good example of someone who hits you with a tsunami of energy and we all know someone who sucks (energy, that is!). They are the ones with the victim attitude that won't let you get a word in edgeways. After visiting them you feel drained, they are like vampires.

Here is an interesting point of view, people with a disease can often be suckers and those with answers, the carers and professionals can be pushers. What is a pusher? Is it someone who wants to sell you something? A car, a political idea, surgery, a service, drugs, a point of view…? Even if you don't require it!

One point of view as to why the body likes to move, what humans call exercise, is to run energy through it. When you are sick the body often cannot move as easily, so energy is unable to move as dynamically. This can slow everything down, creating more pain and suffering. This particular technique can be used before you do any movement (exercise), even if it is just walking to the post box. Doing this twice a day for ten minutes can be of great benefit to the body.

The Thymus exercise.
This exercise is simple and effective. You could do it standing or if, like me, you are a sloth, by lying down. Just imagine for the moment that your arms and legs are spread out and you make a giant cross. Simply ask the energy to flow through your fingers, up the arms and through your thymus, which is just below the notch of where the collar bones meet. Let the energy cross over at this point and flow out of your legs and feet. Now ask for the energy to flow up the feet and legs, cross over at the thymus again and flow out through the arms and fingers. Now ask the energy to flow down through the crown of the head, through the thymus, and out the feet, and then up the feet, through the thymus, and out through the crown. Ask for all four flows to occur simultaneously and say "Thymus exercise run." The purpose of asking you to imagine your body in an "X" shape is so I don't have to draw a diagram. It is NOT so you can imagine or visualize the energy flow. Imagination and visualization are incredibly slow and strengthen your mind, not your awareness. Chances are that you are so fast at this sort of thing that you have always thought there is something wrong with you because you can't visualize. Or you are always three steps ahead of everyone else. Cool hey! You have such a natural talent and ability at playing

with energy that you have been able to create dis-ease in your body. What a creator you are.

Would you like to use that ability to create something new with your body? Would you like a story here? I used this exercise not so long ago. It was the first time in three years that I was able to jog. I jogged a couple of kilometres in the mountainous region of Mt Tamborine on the Gold Coast of Australia. On the last hill I started to flag and so I asked the thymus exercise to run. My knees suddenly came up to my chest as my body propelled me up the hill like a horse. I got to the top of the hill and continued to jog straight past my friend's house for another 500 metres. I laughed and laughed. How does it get any better than that? Even if you are not sick you can use this with any exercise.

Have you bought a point of view that says that a body part is the way it is because of x, y or z? If you have done this you will only be able to find answers that align and agree with that. If this is the case, then you will probably find that your body will display the same symptoms even when you find something that is supposed to relieve that symptom. For example, I was at an Access class and someone said to me that I looked very yellow and suggested that I had a liver function problem. Oh yeah, just because someone has a degree or has done a lot of work on themselves or cured themselves doesn't mean they can't be wrong. This was not a very kind thing to say. There was no question in it, she just wanted to look clever. She was just repeating a point of view she had heard. I got extremely angry at this, so I asked Gary what this was all about. He asked me to ask my body if this was true. No, it was not! I was angry because this person had tried to force her point of view down my throat. I had also had this particular point of view pointed out (I love the way we can manipulate the English language) at least 15 times by others. Just because the majority says it is so does not make it true. Feel the energy. If it is light it is true for you, if heavy it is lie and if it is lie, you can ask some more questions.

The more you claim your ability to direct energy, the more you can choose to do it. All you have to do is ask it to move. 'That sounds too easy," I hear some of you say. "Yeah, okay, I am lying!" Those that think it is too easy, you are right. I am wrong, it is easy! Would you like to claim, own and acknowledge the talent and ability you have of directing energy? Would you like to play with this?

Remember my client with the BMW shirt? We played with this one day. We went to a busy coffee shop. I said, "We are going to practise directing energy. We are going to practise being seen as the magnificent beings we truly are." He looked nervous as he said, "What are we going to do?" I couldn't resist a little joke to make it a little lighter. I said, "We're gonna rob the coffee shop." We laughed. When I explained what we were really going to do he looked paler than when we joked about robbing the place! My client's job was to stand in the middle of the coffee shop and pull the energy of the universe through him and be willing to be seen by everyone. He was to do this until people started to turn around and look in his direction. We laughed a lot afterwards, especially when he asked if I had done it. I couldn't resist another joke and said, "What? Do you think I am that crazy!" Yeah, I have done it. I do it often and I know what my client went through. I know how long it can feel to be standing there. I know all the tricks that he used, that we all use, not to be seen. Like pretending I am waiting for someone. That is not a willingness to be seen. That is weaseling, hiding! We hide because in the past we have bought the point of view that if we really show up as who we truly are, we will be judged and hounded and squashed. Please play with this, the more looks you get, the more energy you are pulling, the more YOU shows up. Are you willing to destroy and uncreate all the points of view that stop you from being seen as you truly are? The less points of view, the less judgements we cram into the body, the less we are the effect of disease, the more at ease our body becomes. Would you like your body at ease? YES, SIR! Oh, yeah! The more you play with it, the more you are aware of when others are doing it. So, when that doctor or therapist tries to sell you something by pushing huge amounts of energy at you, you'll know they are trying to sell you something. You won't buy it unconsciously, you will be able to ask your body if it is true for it, and then choose for you. That choice may be to do the surgery or to walk out of the doctor's office with your intestines intact. There is no such thing as a right or wrong choice, only light or heavy. If it is heavy it is not true for you, if it is light then it is true for you. The great thing about choosing like this is, if it gets heavy later on, choose again. As you become more willing to be you, to be seen, more willing to receive everyone's judgement, you won't care if you keep making different choices. If you use, "Who does this belong to?" with this, you'll also recognise that none of it is yours anyway. How does it get any better than that?

Are you willing to claim, own and acknowledge that you are weird, unique and different and that you don't fit into the box? Yes! Yes! and again, YES! Be you and change the world!

I have a friend called Joy Voeth who has produced a CD called "Access the Joy of Movement" which describes the thymus exercise and many other techniques. If you would like to purchase one you can check it out on the website. www.joylives.com

Tools and Tips
- Try the Thymus exercise. The more you play with energy, the better you get at it.
- If old things, like visualization, are not working for you, bin them.
- Ask your body.
- If you have a pain or a strong emotion we tend to contract in order to focus on it. What if you were to expand instead?
- As a humanoid, you are energy.
- Manipulating energy is easy, if you have bought that it is difficult or you have to be special, then it is a lie. Return it to sender.

Chapter 15

Caring for people who have a dis-ease

If you think nobody cares, try missing a couple of payments.

A teacher noticed that a little boy at the back of the class was squirming around, scratching his crotch, and not paying attention. She went to the back of the class to find out what was going on. He was quite embarrassed and whispered that he had just recently been circumcised and he was quite itchy. The teacher told him to go down to the principal's office.

He was told to telephone his mother and ask her what he should do about it. He did that and returned to the classroom. Suddenly, there was a commotion at the back of the room.

The teacher went over to investigate to find the little boy sitting at his desk with his little private part hanging out.

"I thought I told you to call your mom!" she said.

"I did," he said, "and she told me that if I could stick it out till noon, she'd come and pick me up."

How often do you misinterpret someone? How often do you buy something as real? How much of this book have you misinterpreted?

"You can lead a horse to water but you can't make him drink." By now I would say that you will see this saying as an interesting point of view. Let's break it down, there is a "but" there for starters. Now horses have beautiful butts, but we aren't talking about them! The energy of the word 'but' says, "Hey! What I just said is not really what I think." And in this case it is true you can't lead a horse to water. You could ask the horse to take you to water and it would probably oblige, and the ones you lead without a question, the ones you force, are either going to buck you off or get you back big time in another life! So, this statement could be easily misinterpreted depending on the point of view you have bought.

Oki dokey! So what is the point of the previous story? Here it is. You may have picked up this book for an ailing friend, partner, parent or as a professional for a client, and you have read it and you have gone, "Hey, this is so cool! This will really help. I've gotta get this to them. This will blow their socks off! This could be the change that will get them back onto the road to recovery." You can't lead a horse to water and you can't make them drink. You can't make someone heal if they are not willing. Also, do you have a vested interest? Perhaps you want to prove to them that there is another way? So, you could ask a question, "Do I have a vested interest here? Do I want to save them? Am I proving the rightness of my point of view? Am I doing superiority?" If you are, you are not in allowance of their choice to create their life the way they want it. You are judging and you want something (coming from lack). You could ask them a question, "Hey Pop! I found this interesting book about healing. Would you like a copy?" Pop says, "No thanks, not more mumbo jumbo!" Stop! "Interesting point of view Dad." "Yes please." Give it to them with no investment. How does it get any better than that? Or maybe they ask you, "I don't know what to do." This is a statement, the question part is, "Can you help me?" or "Where can I get help?" or "Where can I go to find out more?" or "How can I heal...?" I know you'll be tempted to ask in a couple of weeks, "How'd that book go?" That is often a vestment in the outcome, especially if you are thinking about it a lot. Is that following the energy? If they start to ask you questions, then you can help. Until then, get out of their kitchen and allow them to cook up their own life. That is being kind. Anything else is shoving your recipe for life down their throat, that is a recipe for disaster (pardon the pun, I'm on a roll, a salad roll). I know, I have been there, done that, got the t-shirt. I did it with my Mum and it was horrid. The day I stopped, she changed. The day I asked her a question was the day our relationship shifted and became so much more interesting, fun. She even uses some of these tools. The day I gave my Dad a copy of Gary's book, "Magic, you are it, be it," he opened it up to the human / humanoid thing, he read that chapter, left it on my bed, got drunk and argued with me about all sorts of things. Hay (pardon the pun again), you can't lead a horse to water and you can't make him drink. You can ask a question, you can be in allowance, you can do the courses or have a session or buy a book or CD, you can change your reality and in changing your reality you change all realities. What are you unwilling to perceive, know, be and receive that if you were willing to perceive, know, be and receive would change all realities?

My ex-wife watched me go from a humanoid dynamo to the ghost who walks. She stuck it out to the end. She cleaned the walls of blood and shit, she held my hand whilst I was dying. She went to work whilst doing all this. One day I came home from a therapy session and a week on my own and I said, "We have to stop. I would like a divorce. We can sell the house and split everything." And she said, "We have to stop. I would like a divorce. We can sell the house and split everything!" almost simultaneously. I went into remission. After ten years of marriage we sold the house, started divorce proceedings and, trying to be nice, my wife said, "You can stay with me until you are better." That divorce turned out to be a "bloody" battle of six months, literally! We thought that by getting divorced we would clear the energy between us. We thought we could continue to help each other, live with each other. It wasn't until we started Access that we realised that we had just shot ourselves in the feet with being nice, and that we had not actually cleared energetically all that sticky stuff that kept us hanging onto each other. Please, I am not asking you to get a divorce. I am using this as an example. What I am saying is, please choose for you, and not choose for the rules, reasons and rightness of the points of view that you have bought. The good news here is we both chose for ourselves to split, and in that choosing, we changed our reality. We got a shit load of money from the sale of the house and I went into remission (practically the next day). The divorce became a bloody battle not because we fought each other, it became bloody because I became sick again, because we decided to try and help each other. Really, we reneged on the choosing for ourselves when Simone offered to let me stay on longer. I even recall saying to her, "Be careful what you say." Did I get better? No, I got worse and worse. You don't have to go there, we did. Please use the awareness we have had from this and choose for you.

Two years later (and the blood count up to normal), I was participating in a group when someone brought up that they didn't want to go home because their ailing partner was waiting for them. There was that "ugh" thing in my universe again. This person didn't want to clear this. He was a person of his word and there was a marriage commitment to uphold! Both lives were hell, because their commitment of marriage led to resentment and hence he thought (thinking is stinking!) he had no choice. This person was not willing to uncreate the commitment, because he thought it would mean breaking his oath. He thought it would mean he would have to leave the other. He thought that staying and creating all the emotional shit was the right thing to do. More likely, the other was dying to get out of this relationship, literally. This person was not willing to even sniff at the infinite possibilities. Was this kind? Staying in a relationship that you resent, to uphold an oath you made 40 years ago, or destroying that oath and choosing to stay or go, because that is what you would like to do, because that is what you would be choosing now?

This "ugh" was a realisation of what my wife was going through whilst caring for me. By now we were divorced. I was still living with her and she was driving to work to escape the situation, and on the way home she was wondering if I was going to be dead or alive. Since then I found out that she was hoping I was dead then it would all be over, have you thought like this? Don't beat yourself up, ask who does this belong to? Or who am I choosing for? I am a little bit Humanoid, so I have a talent of picking up other's thoughts and emotions. What was my wife thinking and feeling? How many other people out there were thinking and feeling similar things? I was picking this up from her, from my Mum, from my sister etc. Thinking they were my own thoughts and feelings and then broadcasting these to my wife, friends, family etc. See where this is going? Blood bath at the Okay Coral. Yes, that is right! Symptoms increased exponentially.

What commitments, oaths, swearings, fealties and vows do you have with the sick person in your life? What are you creating with them? What investment do you have with their sickness? Does it give you control? Is what you are thinking and feeling causing something in their life? Could it limit their capacity to heal? Are you being kind or are you being driven by old patterns? Are you resentful? Are you putting the other person first and is that being kind to you? And if you are not being kind to you, can you be kind to another? Do they really require your help or are you shoving it onto them?

Are you willing to give all that up and destroy and uncreate it?

As a carer what can you do? You can use all the tools in this book, everything that is written here for the sickie in your life can be used by you. And, if you are both willing to do it, wow! What are the infinite possibilities?

Gary runs a class called X-men. This is about children who have been labelled as having a specific ability like A.D.D, autism etc. My point of view is that these kids are often extremely psychic and aware, that they live in a reality devoid of linear time and many Human made limitations hence their "strange" behaviour and we try to squash them into our reality. Being a trained teacher in the area of disability my ears pricked up when Gary told the story of a boy who he had worked with who had the human label of Autism. The young fellow was displaying less "weird" behaviour after a short time with Gary and Dain working with his Mom and him. A few weeks later the Mum was talking to Dain saying that the weird behaviours were returning. Dain asked some questions and discovered that

Mum had been researching more about autism on the internet. Her son had picked up all her thoughts and feelings and pictures she was broadcasting whilst she was researching. Ouch!

When I was deep in the sickness story I was researching books, the internet, people… I was buying so many points of view I became confused. The symptoms became more frequent and intense. You, as carer, may well want to help your patient so you may choose to become a researcher to find some answers. If your patient is Humanoid they may well pick up all this research, what the symptoms look like, worse case scenarios, horrid side effects of drugs and, hey presto! They may take these points of view as their own and pow! You get the picture, the symptoms appear to increase.

What can you do, ask some questions of the universe. What is this about? How is this disease affecting me? For what reason am I doing all this research? Is this being kind? What do I have to prove? What is my vestment in this?

"Destroy and uncreate." You have read this many times already and it is a powerful tool. You can use it every night before bed and destroy and uncreate all the glop and the gloop that you have going on with your client or the person you are caring for. Then each morning you'll have the opportunity to see the client, the person you are caring for anew, because you destroyed all the expectations, all the thoughts and feelings, all the vestment in the relationship. The more aware you become, the greater opportunity your client, friend or relative has to heal. You can be in complete allowance of their choices. Be you and change the world!

There is a process in Access about letting the person choose to die. Yep, that is just what you read. Death is a choice. It is called "Exit Stage Left."

I did this with a plant. I had heard this "money" tree outside a flat, repeatedly call out to me, "Please get me away from here." I thought of stealing it, "POC and POD that" and "Who did that belong to?" It was dying. There was no light, there was no gratitude. There was heaps of expectation on this plant. The person it belonged to had bought the point of view that having a money tree at the front door was going to make her more wealthy. If the state of the plant was an indication of her bank balance I would be surprised if she could afford the rent. Interesting point of view!

So along came me. Self designated saviour of the universe, with Access, with the answer. I just shot myself in the foot! Did I have an investment? Was I going to prove my point of view about Feng Shui being wrong and Access being right? Did the plant become healthier? Interesting point of view I had those points of view. So, in a last ditch attempt I thought of buying new soil for this plant. I was at the checkout when I realised, "I have an investment in healing this plant. Destroy and uncreate that, POD and POC that. Okay, what else is possible?" I put the bag of dirt back on the shelf and when I got home I talked with the plant and said, "I am willing to listen to your requests. I am in total allowance of your choice to stay or die. What will you choose?" The plant said, "Cut everything dead off me." That left a stick about 2 inches long with 2 leaves on it! "Move me there. Put some Xooma on me." (A product that I use in my water to help mineralize and alkalise it). That's what I did. I bet you want to know if it is alive or dead. Do you have an investment in the outcome of this story? I don't. I am in complete allowance of that plant. Are you willing to be in complete allowance of the person you are caring for? Anything that prevents that from happening are you willing to destroy and uncreate that? To POD and POC that?

Okay, I hear you say, "That was just a plant, Humans are more important." Is that true? Is that a judgement? Are you Human? As an infinite being would you do judgement or would you be in total allowance of every one's choice, plant, animal, mineral or "Human"? When an animal's body is in pain and suffering, when it can no longer heal itself, the animal chooses to die. It says, "Okay body, I hear you, there is nothing more that can be done. So I am choosing to let you die and I will get a new body." Your body is an animal. It is more conscious than you, because it doesn't have trillions of years worth of thoughts and feelings to separate it from consciousness.

Here is another great tool: "What is right about this that I am not getting?

As the carer, professional or sickie, have you bought the point of view that the way to fix a problem is to focus on what is <u>not</u> working? Is it no wonder then that when sickness appears in our lives, we often go to the wrongness of the situation, of all the things that are not working, or the wrongness of the body? Is that a judgement? When we focus on the wrongness, on what is not working, then we start making the disease bigger than us. We diminish us. When things appear to be at their lowest there is a tendency to go to what is wrong and try to remove that wrongness. This eats up a huge amount of energy. A question that we can use in this position is, "What is right about this that I am not getting?" This will bring your attention back from the wrongness and open up possibilities that we are unable to think of.

Earlier on in the book I heard some of you ask the question, "Does this stuff work with kids?" The answer is definitely, "Yes!" I bring it up again because this is an appropriate time to tell you a story about a friend and the power of asking questions. I asked her the question, 'What brought you to Access?" That question opened so much up for me and perhaps it will continue to work for millions of others. What are the infinite possibilities? It was this question that led to other questions, which lead to the publication of this book. Her niece has Ulcerated Colitis. She asked me the question, "As an aunt, or grandparent or friend of the family, would you like to have the opportunity to pass on a book like this to the parent of a child with Ulcerated Colitis (or any other disease)?" The answer was, "Yes." She then said something to the effect of, "Then get to it! What if bleeding from your butt was your body's way of getting you to write this book? To expand people's awareness about Ulcerated Colitis?" So with much gratitude to my friend, my body and all those kids and people out there that may benefit from such a book, I have made a demand of myself to get this book out there. What else is possible? This is a great example of how one question can change the world. Please ask questions. Please ask **lots** of questions.

Tools and Tips
- Allow the person their choice.
- Don't buy their story as real.
- Don't push your point of view on to another.
- Be aware of what you are thinking. If you are thinking of pain, suffering and gory, and the person you are caring for is Humanoid, they will think those thoughts are theirs and create from them.
- If someone does not ask a question, they are not interested.
- "Interesting point of view" is the tool to use. Be kind to yourself. If you say it out loud chances are that you will be judged and wear their wrath.
- What if the judgements you have lock others in their story?
- What if the child in your life was so psychic that they were creating disease from the judgements and points of view around them?
- Hey, you are not a door mat. If things are getting ugly, or they just want to load you up with their story, get the hell out of there. Buying their story will only justify their point of view as being right and that is not creating awareness for anyone.

Chapter 16
If it is light

How much deeper would the ocean be without sponges?

Jokes are great because they bring up how absurd our thoughts and limitations really are. If you don't get the joke we say exactly that, "I don't get it." We don't get it because we are so much in our story that we can't see the absurdity of it. Jokes bring up the energy of an idea and when you "get it" you laugh to release the limitation. How cool is that? Every joke is an opportunity to feel lighter. Laughter works because it helps you identify limitations. Hey, it is just an interesting point of view. When we buy into someone's misery, we are not helping them, we are creating more crap. We are aligning and agreeing with their point of view, which in turn validates their disease. When there is lightness in our lives, when we are not buying others points of view, we are not aligning and agreeing, we are not resisting or reacting. By default we see things as they are, "Justin IPOV" (just an interesting point of view), then we can really help. So tell a joke or two. Can't remember any? Highlight the jokes in this book. If they don't get it you know they are not interested in healing. They are interested in the disease, in seriousness, in doom and gloom, and that is their choice. I almost typed that is their "right." Is right a limitation? How many people with disease would rather be right than heal? How many carers or professionals would rather be right than allow another their choice? And if you have done this or are doing this would you be willing to destroy and uncreate it all?

Everything that prevents you from laughing at my jokes, at my sense of humour, at your sense of humour, are you willing to destroy and uncreate that? Perhaps I should have started the book with that clearing!

You may have noticed by now that most of the chapter titles have little jokes as sub-headings. This was designed to make things light. Pain, suffering, gory and disease is all so heavy when we buy in to it. Unconsciousness is heavy, it is serious, it is important, it is significant, it is terminal. Even if your body is dying you can still have a bloody good laugh, you can still be conscious. Whilst I was in my death throws I suddenly became aware of the big joke, the absurdity of all that I had bought. What really did it for me was that I had more money in my bank account than I had ever had in this life and here I was choosing to die. I had spent so much of my life worrying about money, spending it and how to get it, and now that I had it, I was choosing not to use it. I almost died laughing. How does it get any better than that?

To finish this chapter I am going to let Rebecca tell her "story" and how one 'Bars' session changed her life. She is now an Access Learning Facilitator in Sydney.

"I finally experienced Access in January of 2007, after 18 months of invitations and updates. The time was finally right and I went along to a 'Bars' swapping evening, completely unaware of the fact that my whole life was about to change in ways I couldn't possibly imagine.

I had just returned home from my farewell tour. My doctors had advised me that it was time to say good bye to my family and friends. Best case scenario - I had 6 months to live, worst case - less than 3 months. I wasn't even going to make it to my 30th birthday or see my daughter turn 3.

The doctors were baffled. At first, each one would get excited and attempt to solve the mystery. Then after a barrage of painful and invasive procedures, they would all give up and refer me on to someone new. And so, the cycle continued and the testing would begin again.

It seemed as though my body existed purely from pain. Everything, including breathing, was difficult and painful. I was completely exhausted. Often waking to eat, only to find that the effort of actually eating was so exhausting that I would then sleep another 2 hours. To say my life was miserable is an extreme understatement.

As I had my 'Bars' run that first time all I could think was, "Is this going to take much longer?" I just wanted to go home and go to bed. When it was finished, Jessica, my bartender asked, "So, how was that for you?" I thanked her very much and explained that I didn't really feel anything but thanked her kindly for trying.

I then went outside to wait for my husband to pick me up. He was running a little late so I though I'd just start walking. So I walked and I walked and I walked. It wasn't until I was a few kms up the road that I realized, hey, I had walked quite a distance and realised for the first time in many, many years I wasn't in any pain. Then I called my husband and discovered that he had driven right past me, having not seen me, as it was impossible for him to perceive that I could have walked so far.

As you can imagine, we both felt like we had experienced something magical yet wondered how it was possible. The next morning, I tentatively opened one eye and then the other and waited. I couldn't believe it. Nothing! No pain! None! I was ecstatic, beside myself and over the moon. How does it get any better than that? My lovely husband however, was still skeptical. "I'd better not do too much. I had to be careful. Let's just see how you go." But I KNEW. I knew in my whole being that our lives were going to be very different from that day forward. I had made a choice and I had chosen to live and to live well.

What if everything in life was a choice? What are you choosing for yourself? Would you like to be choosing something different? Is your life, as it currently is, enough for you? Do you know that you are capable of more? What would that look like for you?" Thank you, Rebecca.

Wow! "Is it possible that it could be that easy?"

Tools and Tips
- Heaviness is not something that is right or wrong it is just a "stagnation of energy", it just not light.
- Light is not something that is good or bad it is just an energy that you perceive as easy, where you get a sense of fun and enjoyment, or in some cases a wow.
- Neither light or heavy has reason attached to it. It is faster than thought, and it can change over time. Don't make it significant.

Chapter 17

The Lost Chapter – The Be Aware Clause

You can't hide a piece of broccoli in a glass of milk.

The following story is to demonstrate how the tools work in everyday situations and sometimes that things are the opposite of what they appear to be.

The deadline of this book going to print is fast approaching. I am emailing Hong Kong non stop, I am about to put money in their account and I suddenly received an email to hold off until after Chinese New year as paper prices have just changed. Instead of going into frustration over the delay I ask "How does it get any better than that?" In the mean time I have worked out a base price for the book. In doing this I find that with all the customs, freight, taxes, duty and everything else that it is not an easy process. Everything around this has a sense of heaviness. I use the tool "if it is light it's true for you, if it's heavy it is a lie, so ask another question." I ask "what else is possible?" and have an insight to look at the original printer I had connected with in Australia several months ago. The next day they ring me and give me a great price that compares to Hong Kong. How does it get any better than this?

Still there is something heavy around this. I ask the question "what is right about this I am not getting?" and my friend Gabi Plumm, who I am co-authoring a children's book with called "Mumble and Jumble" (about two amazing kids that use these tools in their lives), emailed me information about literary grants. One stipulation being that the book must be a minimum of 30 thousand words. This book runs shy by about a chapter. I have always had the feeling that there was something missing from the book a type of "incompleteness", so I ask the question "is there a lost chapter?" In our correspondence Gabi and I talk about asking our bodies things and there is a realization that a few people's bodies don't respond in the same way as I have described earlier, that sometimes things are the opposite of what they appear. Wow the birth of the lost chapter, "The Be Aware Clause." At no time did I become frustrated, I never came to any conclusion, I made no judgements, I didn't buy anyone's point of view, I didn't stop, I never had a definitive answer to blind me from other possibilities, I just kept asking questions. The whole process was so much fun. I created my life rather than being the effect of life. How cool is that? Did this create dis-ease in my body? Or did it create a sense of lightness and ease for my body and other bodies around me? For those still requiring an answer, it was the latter.

Humanoid bodies are unique; they often don't fit into the form and structure of this linear reality. Pretty much like you, you just don't fit. What if you were to acknowledge that? Every body is going to require different things at different times, have you ever noticed that you will eat a particular food for a period of time and then not touch it again for a while? What if this is your body's way of following the energy? It's weird and that is cool. What if your body's "yes" is not shown by moving forward toward the item, that it was something else for your body? Good question. So here is a possibility. Ask it a question you know is true like am I male or am I female? Do I have a cat? Ask it a question you know it is going to give you a definite "yes" or "no" to. In consciousness, is everything always the same, or is it in a constant state of flux? In consciousness, would it be possible that things could be the opposite of what they appear to be? You are unique and your body is unique, would you be willing to claim, own and acknowledge that?

What if being aware was more expansive than being careful? Does being careful create a sense of always having to be alert that something awful may be just around the corner, a sense of tension, a sense of un-ease, of dis-ease in you and your body? How many times have you asked your son, daughter or partner to be careful? How often has your Mum said to you "be careful dear?" How often has being careful resulted in exactly what you have to be careful about coming to fruition, or created a sense of tension in your day? "Be careful of the used car salesman," does that make you feel light or heavy? "Be careful of the surgeon he only wants to sell you his point of view." Is that heavy or light? Heavy right? You are looking to buy a car and you are looking for everything that is wrong with it, is that fun? You require the skills of a surgeon and you resist and react to every word being said and you leave feeling wiped out, heavy, just plain "yuk". What if being aware required you to ask a question? Could you then ask a question like "what is right about this that I am not getting?" Coooooool question.

Every time someone says "be careful" to you what are you going to do? Will you tell them of your new awareness about what careful creates, or are you going to be aware of what the other can hear? Not many people will give up their point of view without a fight; they will probably resist and react to you if you offer an alternative (unless they have read this book of course). Could you use a tool? What tool could use? Interesting point of view? Wow some of you are getting this. Yahoo.

I don't do careful any more, I be aware. Being aware has an expansion about it, a joy, a sense of fun, a sense of lightness. What if be being careful creates limitation or contraction that inhibits you from perceiving the infinite possibilities, or the future? Like that speeding car heading straight for you. Doing careful is contracting, tension creating, dis-ease creating or has a sense of heaviness with it. What if you were so busy at doing careful, looking left and right when crossing the road you failed to notice the car in the drive way behind you? Ouch. What if every child in the world was asked to be aware rather than careful? Would that make a difference?

Be aware of the words that you are using. What if words helped to create our lives? What if we are using words that don't match up with the energy of expansion and joy, of what we would like to create in our lives? What if we are using words that are limiting, contractive, and heavy that would create more "shit" in our lives? In my case I literally did this. Cute, but not at all bright.

Each word has an energy attached to it, just like "careful" and "aware". Which is lighter for you? The energy of careful is based on the human concept of worry, because our Mums and Dads were worried that we may get hurt. What if our children cut and paste that word "careful" into their lexical repertoire. Then do they also cut and past that energy in to their bodies? Have you done that? Has that been contributing to your dis-ease? Everywhere you have bought being careful would you be willing to destroy and uncreate all that?

Would you like some other words to play with?:

Want – means to lack. Every time you say or think it "I want to get better," the universe hears "I lack getting better" and supplies you with that, ouch. Every time you say "I want a new Mercedes," what does the universe hear? "I lack a new car." Is that why you are still running around in that old bomb?

Try – the energy attached to this is; "I'm not really going to do it." When someone says to you in that defensive tone "I am trying my best," are they or are they just "trying" your patience?

But – well if you have read previous chapters you already know my point of view about butts. Cute.

Need – need will always lead to greed. It has a victim energy attached to it. It implies that we have no choice, that we are the effect of life, not the creator of life.
What would you like to be? The energy behind this word does not honour the abundance of the universe, instead it creates a poverty consciousness.

There are lots of others. If you would like to, treat yourself to a new dictionary and play with the energy of words. Find one printed before 1947 as these have a truer meaning of words. On second thoughts don't do that, it may give you the possibility to change.

Be aware that it is the energy behind the word that counts. What would it be like if you were to be aware of every word that comes out of your mouth or rattles around in your brain? Would that make a difference? With this knowledge you may like to re-read the book and be aware of the words that have been used, and how they have been put together. Or not. Read it with awareness and you and your cute little body will become more aware of the energy behind it. The expansiveness, the fun I had in writing the book, the lightness. What if this energy is the energy you are "seeking" in-order for your body to be at ease? Everywhere you have compared this book with others and come to the conclusion that this book has nothing new in it, would you be willing to destroy and uncreate all that? "Read" the energy of the book, and you may see that the lexical arrangement and usage is somehow different. You may start to perceive a change in energy, a lightness of being, or even an ease with your body. Perhaps you have already encountered this, a little giggle, a laugh out loud, a light bulb going off, a relaxation. What was it for you? And will you acknowledge that in you and in your body? Will that make more ease for your body? What else is possible?

Tips and Tools
- Your body is unique.
- Some things can be the opposite of what they appear to be. If you are getting weird responses with your body when using the "ask your body" technique, ask it a question you know is true for you to find out what is a "yes" and "no" for your body.
- Be aware, not careful.
- The words we speak and think carry an energy and create our lives. Be aware of the words you use. Words to watch out for are; want, but, try, careful and need.

Post Script and Contact Details

Please don't trust me, please don't trust anyone. The only person you can trust is yourself. Don't make this another doctrine, another answer. Please remember, this book is just an introduction, it is not the answer. If you were to use "interesting point of view" for everything in this book, you will not buy into anything that is not true for you. Ask questions of the universe and yourself and others and your body. If it does not feel light it is not true for you. If it feels heavy, it is a lie or there is a lie attached to it. Anything that this brings up, let us destroy and uncreate that. Good, bad, right, wrong, POD, POC, all 9, short boys and beyonds.

I am grateful to you for buying this book and being willing to show up as the magnificent being you truly are. Thank you for being you.

Whatever you choose to do with the questions and tools that are presented here may that choice be expansive for you. **May all of life come to you with ease, joy and glory!**

PPS: The plant chose to die.

For more Information, to purchase other products, course enquiries, private sessions, Bars sessions and body work:

Liam: (+ 61) 0429806196
liamrphillips@yahoo.com
www.liamphillips.com
www.accessconsciousness.com
www.mumbleandjumble.com
www.goodvibesforyou.com

Testimonials

"Having had the privilege of reading Liam's book I could see how much the tools of Access Energy Transformation have changed his life and his body.

Knowing a little about his journey during this illness I can so appreciate the ups and downs he went through and his total dedication to using the tools that would allow him to communicate and understand his body's requirements. It is an entertaining and heartfelt read which had me laughing and sniffling, as well as nodding in recognition all the way through.

Liam has a talent for putting his thoughts on paper in a no-nonsense, 'get over yourself' sort of way that I perceive will endear him to many who are having difficulties with their bodies in any form.
Thanks Liam, a great read, what else is possible?"

Gabi Plumm, *Author of Registered Under Another Name and co-author with Liam Phillips of The Extraordinary Adventures of Mumble and Jumble.(soon to be released).*

"This book is absolutely amazing!! A MUST for anyone who's ever felt ill, been sick or had a pain in their body. He's also talking to carers which is great as they can facilitate and empower those they care for and give them a different possibility, if they are willing to receive it.

Liam looks at dis-ease from a completely different point of view. He acknowledges that his body would like to be acknowledged; would like to be asked where it would like to go, what it would like to eat and so on. "If it involves your body, ask it!" Simple, yet most of us don't do it or have some excuse why we don't.

I was fortunate enough to do some work with Liam and the changes that occurred for him and his body when he acknowledged that he is the creator of his body and also of his dis-ease were absolutely awesome!! Thank you, Liam for allowing me to be a part of your story!!

There is so much information here and many, many tools you can use to create ease with your body. Oh and great jokes (who says information has to be serious?). One of my favourite bits is the Dogs Diary!! What's your favourite thing?

Looking forward to seeing you on Amazon and in every bookstore!! How does it get any better than this?"

She also pre ordered 10 copies

"Liam's story (book) was and is such an inspiration to me for the willingness he actually has to choose life in the face of death. Imagine being given an either or choice? Life or death? This book offers you a completely irregular way to look at life, and the way you are living it. Does anyone really know what is going on with our bodies? A very informative, light, humorous, intelligent read. If you wish to know more about how to create a communion with your body and not take it all so seriously, then read this book."

Simone Milasas, Brisbane, Australia.

"I was around when Liam was knocking on Heavens door. I reckon this is the reply he got:

'**We're not ready for you yet,** in fact there are heaps of people we're not ready for yet. Why don't you grab this tool box, use it to heal yourself, then share it around. That would certainly help to lighten our workload.'

This book contains that toolbox

Thank you Liam for sharing it."

Yakov Morris, Cairns, Australia.

Watch out for my next book "Mumble and Jumble" Co-authored with Gabi Plumm. About two kids, their friends and family that use these tools to create their lives. It's fun, exciting, educational, full of tools, and tackles some of life's more challenging issues from some very different points of view.
www.mumbleandjumble.com or visit my web site.
What else is possible?